THE CIVIL WAR

A unit study complete with a timeline, charts, puzzles, graphs, newspaper assignments, fun facts, and more!

Written by Pat Wesolowski

COVER DESIGNED BY
BOBBY MAYER
The Image Company

PHOTOGRAPHS BY
RYAN SMITH

D. P. & K. Productions

Copyright © Pat Wesolowski 1996
April 1996, first printing

All rights reserved. No part of this work may be reproduced or transmitted in any form or by any means, electronic or mechanical, including photocopying, recording, or any information storage and retrieval system. Exceptions are as follows: photocopying is hereby permitted for family and classroom use, by a reviewer or with permission in writing from the publisher.

D. P. & K. Productions
2201 High Road
Tallahassee, Florida 32303
(904) 385-1958

Printed in the United States of America

Other books by Pat Wesolowski:

BIG Ideas/Small Budget
Information, Please! - Beginning Level
Information, Please! - Intermediate Level
Information, Please! - Advanced Level

Foreword

Have you ever looked at an old photograph, or an antique tintype of an historic battle scene, and have your imagination race back to that time? Did it make you feel like you could almost reach out and touch someone there . . . or almost smell the smoke-filled air of the battlefield . . . or hear the enormous crash of shot and shell? Can you imagine trying to see through eyes brimming with tears, as your father, brothers, and friends are lying dead from wounds received while fighting for their country's cause? Have you ever, just for that moment, that small split second of time, felt like you could have been there? If your answer is yes, then you have it! That special spark, that unique gift of an active imagination that can transform the study of history from something old, dry, and dead to something alive, personal, and important for yourself and your family.

I can remember so clearly struggling through an American history textbook while in school . . . as enjoyable as chewing sawdust. Somewhere back in time "experts" replaced the fine art of family history-telling with textbooks and classrooms. But it hasn't always been this way. There was a time when families gathered around and listened while the grandparents told stories of their grandparents and remembered the powerful events that shaped our nation's course. They discussed the events and issues of the day, their causes, and the inevitable consequences. This provided a sense of continuity for their grandchildren. History mattered. It was important. It was personal. Children would hear of their family's history and know they were a part of it. It was a matter of family pride, and they, in turn, would continue to carefully and reverently pass on those stories to the next generation.

This book was prepared with a renewed look at how history should be shared in this personal, family way. By using it you will undoubtedly enjoy a deeper understanding of one of the most emotional and monumental historic events of our young nation.

It has been only one hundred and thirty-one years since "The War" came to a close at Appomattox Court House in Virginia. One hundred and thirty-one years is not that long ago in the short life of our nation, yet the consequences of this historic time are still being felt by all of us every day. Our founding fathers would be shocked to see how our government has grown to the point that its policies touch our lives from the cradle to the grave.

More books and articles have been written about these four short years of war than any other event in our history. The war involved more than 10,000 battles and skirmishes, while killing over 600,000 men and boys for what they believed to be their own just causes. Some were fighting to compel a voluntary union; some for emancipation of the slaves; others for the right to govern themselves in their own states without interference from any outside government. Cries of "preserve the Union" and "down with the Rebellion" versus "state's rights" and "a war for Southern independence" rang loudly throughout the land. Shouts of anger turned to acts of violence.

Americans were killing Americans. This was a very tragic, yet heroic and deeply spiritual time for our nation. The issues and principles mattered deeply to them — they should matter to us. They were important to them, enough to lay down their lives for — they must stay important to us.

Whether you are a beginner or a long-time student of this period, this book will provide you and your family with a helpful guide for preserving accurate history. May your lives be forever enriched through a genuine appreciation of our country's history.

For the sake of our heritage,

Bob Farewell

ACKNOWLEDGMENTS

Where do I begin? I guess alphabetically will be the safest way to thank the following families for their willingness to take part in our Civil War unit study. Without the combined efforts and brainstorming done with these moms, our unit study would not have been near the success that it was. Many, many thanks to Cathy Balentine, Bethany Barnard, Suzanne Farrar, Anita Loizeaux, Sallie Powell, Julie Purvis and Cheryl White. And of course, without the children, there never would have been the need for this cooperative study. Thank you Tiffani, Danielle and Johnny Balentine; Richard, Jeffrey, Millie and Chris Barnard; Sarah Summers and Rachel Farrar; Chris, Matt, Marie and Drew Loizeaux; Tiffany and Bethany Powell; Megan Purvis; Christina White; and Kelley, Stacey, Tony, David, Jonathan, Kimberly and Matt Wesolowski.

I also wish to thank both Bob and Tina Farewell, whose love for books is so evident to all whom they selflessly help, guide and instruct at the many curriculum fairs they attend. Bob has not only studied the War Between the States (his title of preference) extensively, but he is also a reenactor and actually played a small part in the movie *Gettysburg*. His foreword to this study is very much appreciated.

Ryan Smith, a 14-year-old homeschool student, receives credit for most of the great pictures on the cover and throughout the book. Ryan's talent was guided by Ralph Smith, (a Civil War reenactor and professional photographer we met during our study). With their combined effort, these two produced just the type of pictures we wanted. Thanks to both of you and to the children who were more than willing to be dressed for these pictures in period costumes.

My proof readers - what can I say? If you find any errors, it's their fault? If I say that I'm afraid I will lose the ability to convince <u>anyone</u> to proof read any of my future texts. Instead, I'll take the blame for any errors that still exist when this goes to press. All joking aside, Bethany Barnard, Lucy DeCosmo, Anita Loizeaux, and Debbie Pratt deserve more than words can express. Thanks to all of you.

Don, my husband, my final editor (also affectionately known as my "predator"), deserves a special commendation. Many of his suggestions were incorporated into the final publication of this book. It is not an easy task to hand over your manuscript over to someone; asking for his opinions, criticisms, and suggestions. Don did make this fairly painless as his suggestions for changes were always surrounded by praise and adulation (after all, he still has to live with me). He did all of this when his schedule was so full that the only time left in his "day" was after midnight. What love and dedication. May he be served breakfast in bed for the rest of the year (or at least through next week)!

INTRODUCTION

History. If you're like me, when you reflect back on your college and high school years, there is a word that comes to mind when recalling the subject of "History." That word is "boring." History was just another subject to endure, facts to temporarily memorize in order to pass a test, and endless pages of assigned text to read. *Excuse me, I feel a yawn coming on.* I hate to admit it, but it wasn't until my sister-in-law introduced me to historical fiction that I began to not only enjoy history but to appreciate its worth and actually become anxious to learn more. I read Bodie Thoene's *Zion Chronicle* and *Zion Covenant* series almost non-stop. Gilbert Morris' *House of Winslow* series sparked a desire within me to study American history. Comparing a copy of Miles Standish's journal with what I learned after reading the first few books in the *House of Winslow* series made me realize two things: 1) The House of Winslow books were historically accurate; and 2) It was a lot more interesting to read Morris' writings than the journal of Miles Standish.

When studying history, there are so many superior alternatives to using fact-laden text books that history need never be boring again. Most children love to have biographies read to them. Visiting museums and historical places of interest bring history to life. By selecting a particular period of history and incorporating the studies of science, literature, geography, statistics, art, home economics, and more, you will create an enthusiasm for studying history and therefore advance the retention of facts without rote memorization.

This year our family joined seven other families in the study of the Civil War. We learned much more than if we had restricted our studies solely to text books. The following unit study successfully integrates the major disciplines in such a way that it makes learning history enjoyable. Although I like teaching via the unit study method, I am acutely aware of how much time it takes to prepare a quality unit study. Realizing the sustained interest in the Civil War and knowing that most families and teachers would prefer to "teach and learn" rather than "research and prepare"; I have attempted to put it all together in a way that I trust will make studying the Civil War easy, enjoyable and meaningful. When you realize how many books have been written about the Civil War, you become aware that this is a study that could be drawn out for years, if so desired. With the recommendations of the parents who were involved in this study, as well as those of Bob Farewell (owner of Lifetime Books and Gifts), the bibliography has been restricted to books that are essential to making this a great, albeit concise, unit study.

This course could be done individually within the family, but I highly recommend that you join in this adventure with several other families if at all possible. Because group discussion stimulates interest, this publication is ideal for classroom instruction. Our group met once a week to share orally the assignments completed (Speaking 101), read to the children excerpts from literature (Literature 101), published a weekly newsletter (Journalism 101), completed a craft (Art 101), tasted foods from this period (Home Economics 101), listened to a clip of music popular during the war (Music Appreciation 101), and completed other activities. Several adults were assigned a particular subject which they were to prepare and teach when we met each week.

This unit study centers around several major battles which took place during the war. Weekly assignments are to be given to each student relating to the particular battle or period of time that you are presently covering. After completion, the assignments are compiled into a newsletter. The articles are to be written from a "you-were-there" perspective. Topics include everything from "a view from a Northern/Southern leader," "current events," "economic report," "obituaries," and more. In completing the assignments, many subjects are integrated into the weekly newsletter (composition, vocabulary, spelling, and research).

The children are encouraged to divide into teams and have a debate — one side taking the Northern view and one side taking the Southern view. There is a list of questions and answers that the children can study for a "quiz bowl" in Chapter 13. A summary of major battles and a chart with blank spaces is included requiring the children to supply specific information as the study progresses. Each child should make a notebook in order to keep track of all the materials completed personally by him or her. Numerous puzzles, graphs, and quizzes are available to be used as supplemental teaching tools. You will also find a list of interesting facts, as well as suggested field trips. Separate chapters include economics and statistics, geography, crafts, cooking, music and movies. Creating a timeline will pull the entire study together and facilitate retention in your child's mind.

All ages may participate in this study, but we found that most students below age nine didn't really grasp a full understanding of the materials covered. They did, however, enjoy taking part. Our son Jonathan, for example, didn't want to be "out done" by his older siblings when they memorized the *Gettysburg Address* as part of an assignment. For several days the older kids continuously recited this masterpiece to anyone who would listen. "Four score and seven years ago our fathers brought forth to this continent a new nation . . . " became ingrained in our minds. Six-year-old Jonathan amused us all with his rendition of the *Gettysburg Address* that he had memorized, to wit: "Four score and seven years ago, our daddies brought forth cotton to this nation." Memories and experiences like these are some of the intangibles that made this unit study more enriching. Please share with me some of your experiences (as well as comments and suggestions) as you complete this excursion into our country's rich past. Enjoy!

Fort Tallahassee - 1996

Table of Contents

Foreword III

Acknowledgements V

Introduction VI

1. Background Information 1

2. The Newsletter 5

3. Summary of Major Battles 17

4. Creating a Timeline 43

5. Let's Debate the Issues 55

6. Geography 59

7. Literature and Language Arts 65

8. Economics and Statistics 69

9. Interesting Facts and Famous People 79

10. Crafts, Cooking, Music and Movies 95

11. Puzzles, Games and Codes 101

12. Fieldtrips and Activities 127

13. Quiz Bowl Questions 135

14. Bibliography 147

BACKGROUND INFORMATION
CHAPTER 1

Let's begin with a little quiz to see how much you know about the Civil War. This is a true or false quiz. Choose the answer which you think applies:

1. The primary issue over which the Southern states seceded was slavery.

2. General Robert E. Lee was a Southerner who owned many slaves.

3. General Ulysses S. Grant abhorred slavery and had nothing to do with the practice.

4. President Lincoln was a strong abolitionist and his priority was providing freedom for all slaves.

5. The Emancipation Proclamation, issued by Lincoln, freed the slaves in every state.

6. The Northern states had very little to do with the importation, selling or owning of slaves in the United States.

7. At the beginning of the Civil War, the importation of slaves was legal and the South was responsible for importing the majority of the slaves who came into our country.

8. *Uncle Tom's Cabin* accurately portrayed the treatment of the majority of the slaves in the Southern states.

9. Slaves were so inexpensive (and therefore expendable) that their owners were prone to harsh treatment, and not concerned whether they became unfit for labor.

10. The Southern states were the first of the United States to form a Confederacy and threaten secession from the Union.

It may amaze you to know that <u>all</u> of the preceding statements are false. To say I was surprised about the many inaccuracies which I had been taught would be an understatement. I grew up believing that everything I read was not only objectively reported, but true. Sounding a little cynical, I now believe objective reporting is an oxymoron. As long as humans do the reporting, all reporting will, to some extent, be subjective, biased, and otherwise tainted because of the frailties endemic in human nature. If you do not agree with this, you may change your mind after reading differing accounts of the same battles or other conflicting reports of the Civil War. Every attempt has been made to be objective when citing factual information which I deem pertinent in this study of the Civil War. I am certain that some will disagree with my findings. However, I believe that all information provided is correct.

First of all, let's discuss the correct name of this war. This conflict is commonly known to most of us as "the Civil War." Many Southerners recoil at this term and would prefer the title "the War Between the States." The official title used by the Federals is "the War of Rebellion." There were many, many other titles given to this war such as: "the War for Constitutional Liberty," "the War for Southern Independence," "the War for States' Rights," "Mr. Lincoln's War," "the Southern Rebellion," "the Second War for Independence," "the Brothers' War," "the War of Secession," "the Yankee Invasion," "the War for Separation," and others including "the Uncivil War." For the sake of consistency and because it is the most commonly known title, I will refer to this war as "the Civil War."

In many books that I read, the armies are even called by different names. The Northern army is referred to most often as the *Union* or the *Federals*. The Southern army is usually called the *Confederates* or the *Rebels*. Again, for the sake of consistency and for the ease of understanding the information presented, I will refer to the armies as the Northern army and the Southern army.

I strongly recommend that you read at least one of the following books: *The Coming of the Glory* or *Facts The Historians Leave Out* (Tilley, John S.; Tennessee: Bill Coats, Ltd., 1949). The latter is a much shorter and more concise summary of the former, but both of these books reveal many facts and issues to which most of us were never

Background Information — 3 — Chapter 1

exposed in our study of the Civil War. Although I might not agree entirely with every conclusion made by this author, the majority of his findings are indisputable.

Summarizing in these few pages the causes attributed to the Civil War is something that I am unable to do, but has been covered extensively in *Facts the Historians Leave Out*. To discover that New England states had formed a Confederacy and urged secession from the Union prior to the Civil War was unknown by me. I was equally amazed to find out the following:

The Northerners were largely responsible for bringing the slaves into the United States.

The slaves were not kidnapped but were purchased from their tribes with whiskey.

Huge profits were made by the Northerners from the sale of the slaves to the Southerners.

Many of the so called abolitionists in the North did, in fact, play a huge part in funding <u>and</u> profiting from the sale of the slaves.

The economy of the North did not rely on slave labor. For this reason the Northerners could sell the slaves to the South and then nobly say that they were opposed to slavery.

Even when the importation of slaves became illegal, many boats were outfitted for the purpose of smuggling slaves into the United States; most of the owners of these boats being Northerners.

Although the North took a strong stand on the total abolition of slavery, there was no offer made to recompense the slave owners for their purchases.

Immediately prior to the Civil War, slaves were very expensive. Some were purchased for over $1,000 each. This was not a paltry sum in those days!

Only one of every six white men in the South was an owner of slaves.

Long before the Civil War, Robert E. Lee had freed his slaves. At the beginning of the war, Ulysses S. Grant was an owner of slaves.

The slaves were generally very well treated because the owners could ill-afford to jeopardize their large investments. In fact, when there was work to be done that would endanger the health or safety of slaves, their owners would often instead hire cheap, replaceable laborers.

Lincoln, as a Congressman in 1847, is quoted as saying the following: "Any people, anywhere, being inclined and having the power, have the right to rise up and shake off the existing government, and form a new one that suits them better. This is a most valuable, a most sacred right, a right which we hope and believe is to liberate the world."

Although Lincoln was not in favor of slavery, he had seriously questioned the right of the people of the free states to interfere with existing slavery in the South. It was his opinion that the Constitution recognized and protected this institution. His desire was to keep the states united in order to preserve the Union. He was in favor of freeing the slaves if it would save the Union. However, he emphatically denied that the ultimate extinction of this institution was the object of this war.

The Emancipation Proclamation was not an act motivated by a desire to free slaves. It was simply a military strategy that Lincoln used in order to bring the war to an end. If his desire was truly to free the slaves, then he would have freed ALL of the slaves and not just those residing in the states that seceded from the Union. Lincoln abolished slavery where he was utterly without power to do so and yet he allowed it where he had the full authority to abolish it!

Woodrow Wilson is quoted in *History of the American People* as saying of the Emancipation Proclamation, "It was necessary to put the South at a moral disadvantage by transforming the contest from a war waged against states fighting for their independence into a war waged against states fighting for the maintenance and extension of slavery, by making some move for the emancipation as the real motive of the struggle." Obviously this tactic worked. Ask ten people for the cause of the Civil War and you will invariably get, if not a unanimous response, a majority answering "slavery."

As confusing as this may seem for you at the beginning of this study, I do believe that this new information will make your study even more interesting. Regardless, I hope this study challenges you to make the Civil War a fun and informative learning experience for your students.

THE NEWSLETTER
Chapter 2

The glue that binds this study together is the newsletter that your student(s) will publish. Children enjoy seeing their names in print, and knowing that their assignments are going to be published encourages a job well done.

The date on the front of the newsletter will be the period of the war that you are studying. Have the children select a name for their newsletter. They should write their assignments in the first person, as if they were living during the period about which they are writing. A list of possible assignments and a sample newsletter is included at the end of this chapter.

Before you begin the study, decide how often you will publish your newsletter. Weekly is adequate yet not too burdensome. If you are completing this study in ten weeks, you may want as many as ten newsletters. The students will receive their assignments and then submit their completed work for inclusion in the upcoming newsletter. When our group met on Mondays the children orally shared their completed assignments from the week before, received a copy of the most recent newsletter and were given assignments to complete for our next Monday's meeting. During the week I compiled the assignments into the newsletter and distributed it at our next meeting.

If you have access to a computer with a CD Rom, I highly recommend you use the Learning Company's software entitled "Student Writing and Research Center." This software not only combines word processing and publishing, but it includes a copy of *Compton's Concise Encyclopedia* as well. It has a format for newsletters that automatically sets up the design that will be used. If you do not have a student sufficiently experienced with computer skills, then have a parent/teacher publish the newspaper. Although *Compton's* is not my favorite encyclopedia, it does contain a fair amount of Civil War information (including pictures, which can be used in the newsletter when you have a blank space to fill). If you do not have access to a computer or even a typewriter, then the articles may be handwritten. The illustrations may be drawn, cut-out, and then pasted onto a sheet before photocopying.

In the event that you are using this unit study with only one or two students, it might be preferable to combine their assignments into a few newsletters rather than completing one each week. Then again, if this unit study is being used as the majority of the children's school work, they can complete enough varied assignments to fill a weekly newspaper. Our newsletters were typically 4-6 pages long. However, there is no reason why yours could not be as short as one page.

Check with your local libraries (including state and university) in order to find out how far back their newspapers on microfiche date. Our state library has copies of papers dating as far back as the 1800's. They will allow you to use their microfiche machines to view these papers and to copy pages off the microfiche without charge. This is a great learning opportunity and it will give the children a chance to view a real newspaper from the period. If you obtain a copy of *Civil War Times, The Civil War News* or *Camp Chase Gazette*, all currently-issued Civil War periodicals, you will discover them to be full of interesting articles, advertisements, and photographs. These publications are listed in the bibliography (chapter 14) so you can contact them for a sample copy or subscription.

Included in this chapter is a list of many suggestions from which you may choose when giving assignments to your student(s). At the beginning of our unit study, the children wanted to be given specific assignments. As the study progressed, however, most of the children found particular areas of interest and they no longer needed to be assigned a topic. There is at least one advantage in assigning topics: you will have a well-rounded newsletter without having an overabundance of almost identical articles. Also, if you rotate the available topics among the children, they will become exposed to writing about varied subject from many different points of view. Do not feel that you are limited to these suggestions or that you need to include an article from each perspective in every newsletter.

Assignments for the Newsletter

Overview of the Battle
Southern Soldier's View
The Southern Leader
The Northern Leader
Northern Soldier's View
Medical News
Current Events
Economic News
Inventions
Obituaries
Topography and Weather
Scouts and Spies
Illustrators and Photographers
Excerpts from Diaries, Letters or Literature
Artillery and Munitions
Advertisements
Wanted Posters
Prison Report
Tales of a Deserter
View from a Slave
View from Boys and/or Girls
View from a Freed Slave
A Woman's View
Recipes
Songs, Bands and Music
Uniforms and Supplies
Ancestral History

You Snooze, You Lose,
The Civil War News
(Sample Volume)
April 1861 - April 1865

Stephens Receives Letter From Lincoln
By Richard Barnard

On December 22, 1860, Abraham Lincoln wrote to Alexander H. Stephens of Georgia. Lincoln wrote this letter because Georgia might leave the Union. Lincoln thought this could happen because S. Carolina had already seceded on 20 December. In his letter, Lincoln tries to convince Stephens that he will not interfere with Georgia and their slaves. The letter reads, "Do the people of the South really entertain fears that a Republican administration would, directly or indirectly, interfere with their slaves, or with them about their slaves? If they do, I wish to assure you, as once a friend, and still, I hope, not an enemy, that there is no cause for such fears."

Let's hope that Lincoln can convince Georgia and other slave states that he's not a bad President

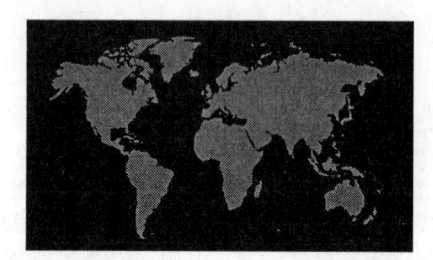

Hot, Humid and Muddy
By Stacey Wesolowski

Soldiers are now in Virginia approaching a place called Manassas. It's very hot - about 86 degrees. There are miles of rolling hills, tangled woods and marshy ravines. The soldiers have to cross over many streams.

A Southern troop came upon a creek with ankle-high water. There was a log across the creek. The soldiers were sitting on the bank taking their shoes and socks off in case they fell in while crossing. The commander wanted to know why the troops were moving so slowly. To his surprise, he found hundreds of soldiers taking off their shoes and socks. The commander got mad and made them put their shoes and socks back on and trudge through the creek.

REWARD

Maryland offers $12,000 to the one who catches **HARRIET TUBMAN!**

Described as a black fugitive slave, and a master of disguises.

DEAD OR ALIVE!

$12,000 REWARD!

Women Involved in the Battle
By Christina White

Many women are becoming involved in this Civil War both at home and in the communities.

Clara Barton, the founder of the Red Cross is helping with the distribution of supplies for the soldiers. (You can be involved in that also if you feel led by sending her clothes, blankets, and canned foods.)

Women are working as nurses also, helping on the fields and in the shelter buildings, trying to help patients recover quickly, so they can get them back in to the war if possible. Other women and their families stand at their gates and wave U.S. flags to the troops, trying to support them.

These women are playing an important role, even though they aren't fighting. They are helping with other aspects, trying to bring us all together.

ARMS IN BABES
By Richard Barnard

It seems young boys are fighting in the war. Even though both the Union and the Confederacy have rules that you must be eighteen or older to enter in the war, boys are lying about their age so they can fight. There is no easy way to check their real age. If the boys are tall for their age they can easily join. Otherwise the recruiters put the boys in the band, usually as a drummer.

Apparently, Johnny Clem ran away and is now a drummer at the age of eleven. Johnny Clem is just one example of the young boys now in the field. These boys are looking for an adventure that will get them away from their chores at home. It's a shame these boys are risking their lives at such a young age.

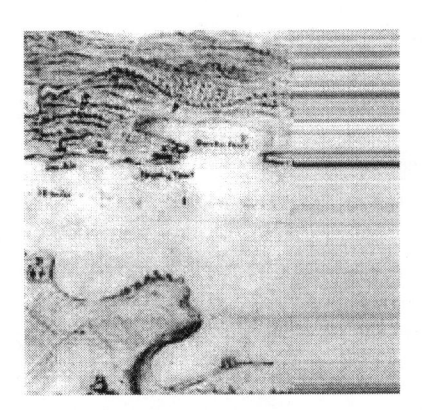

A Strange Sight to See
By David Wesolowski

In June of 1861 a giant balloon called the "Enterprise" was filled with gas and floated over Washington D.C. Attached to the balloon was a thin wire so they could send a message from the balloon to President Lincoln. The inventor of the balloon was Dr. Thaddeus Lowe. The first message to the President said:

Sir: This point of observation commands an area nearly 50 miles in diameter. The city, with its girdle of encampments, presents a superb scene. I have pleasure in sending you this first dispatch ever telegraphed from an aerial station . . . .
T.S.C. Lowe

Ships Battle - Neither Win
By David Wesolowski

It was a cold Sunday morning in Virginia. The water was calm when the *Virginia* and the *Monitor* (both ironclads) started fighting. They were so close to each other that they actually touched. The *Monitor* wasn't able to hurt the *Virginia* anymore so they quit shooting at them. The *Virginia* was so badly damaged from ramming the *Cumberland* the day before that it sailed away for repairs.

* * * *

Diary of Mary Chestnut
By Danielle Ballentine

Mary Chestnut, wife of James Chestnut, former U. S. Senator of S. Carolina, and longtime friend of Jeff Davis and his wife, has these words to say:

We are separated because of incompatibility of temper. We are divorced North from South because we hate each other so.

Whoa to those who began this war, if they were not in bitter earnest.

Every day regiments march by, Charleston is crowded with soldiers. These new ones are running in fairly. They fear the war will be over before they get site of the fun. Every man from every country precinct wants a place in the picture.

Not by one word or look can we detect any change in the demeanor of the Negro slave. They make no sign. Are they stupid? Or wiser than we are, bidding their time.

* * * *

Deserters Run Rampant
A Report by Chris Loizeaux

A young drummer boy, by the name of Irving Fryar, deserted his post in the middle of the Battle of Bull Run, when a Confederate soldier was about to turn him into a cutlass shish kabob. At that instant the boy dropped his drum set and sprinted off into the woods. (On the way into the woods he ran head first into a tree). He was later seen by two officers and was said to be playing with dolls. They had pity and didn't arrest him because they supposed he had brain damage from running into the tree.

* * * *

A Report From Antonia Ford
By Stacey Wesolowski

Hi! My name is Antonia Ford. I'm just a teenager but I have decided to be a spy for the Rebels. I can figure out the exact road plans of the northern troops just by watching their troops. A few days ago I saw some soldiers and found out they were going to attack the confederate troops at Bull Run. I ran six miles, got on a horse and brought my Aunt to go warn General P.G.T. Beauregard. Instead of saying, "Thank you.", he put me in jail. He thought I was a union spy. Well, I convinced him that I am for the Rebels and I'm going to keep on spying for them.

Confederate Receipt Book

A Compilation Over one Hundred Receipts

Adapted To The Times

West & Johnson Richmond 1822

G. W. Gary

$1.03

Matt Loizeaux

A Medical Report
By Megan Purvis

In this report I will tell about the three main diseases that killed two times the amount of people killed in battle. Also I will tell you about a couple of the important people that made medical history. You will also hear about the hospital situation during this war.

The first main disease was Dysentery. Dysentery is an inflammation to the intestine. This causes severe form of stomach upset, and painful cramps. Many soldiers died from this because they became dehydrated. The second major disease is Malaria, a parasite entering the bloodstream caused by the bite of a mosquito. The symptoms are chills, headache, weakness, and an enlarged spleen. The third disease is Typhoid; this disease is from contaminated water supply. This causes fever, drowsiness, headache, and loss of appetite.

The hospitals are ships, barges or regular buildings converted for medical use. There are many temporary facilities set up near or on the battlegrounds. Dorothy Dix, the Superintendent for the U. S. nurses, recruited thousands of "plain looking women" to tend to the sick. Doctors do not seem to know, or understand the importance of sanitation, a balanced diet, and the sterilization of medical examining rooms. The idea of ambulances started during this war with the first horse-drawn ambulance.

There were many important people that took take care of the sick. Mary Walker, a surgeon with the Union Army, is the only woman to receive the Medal of Honor. Clara Barton, known as "Angel of the Battlefield", is the founder of the Red Cross.

With the selected resources, the hospitals are able to save many soldiers.

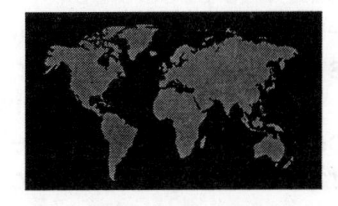

In the News . . .
A Report by Kelley Wesolowski

During the year 1862 the Civil War is probably one of the main things that people are interested in. At least that's what you would think but actually there are many new and exciting things happening all over the world.

This year Victor Hugo has finished his book, *Les Miserables*. It is so popular with the soldiers that they have been calling Robert E. Lee's troops, "Lee's Miserables".

Also this year:
* R. J. Gatling has constructed the ten barrel gun.
* The English cricket team is touring Australia for the first time.
* American author Henry David Thoreau has passed away.
* Lion Foucault has successfully measured the speed of light.
* Swiss humanist Jean Henri Dunant has proposed the foundation of the Red Cross.

Copy Book Found in Negro Woman's Possession
Report by Sarah Summers

"That wars been goin on fer bout a year now. Them soliers come round here looking fer food cuz theres been a shortage. My massa he sends um on there way with bread n gruel. I wouldn't giv um nothin them rebals. Theys campin round these here parts n i don't care fer um. They take peples crops n cows like them there own. They rude rowde n lowd. Is be glad wen theys gon."

* * * *

Shiloh - Battle, Entertaining?
By Rachel Farrar

I went to the battle thinking it would be delightful entertainment. What I saw was people being killed all over because they didn't have on uniforms and they didn't know who was on who's side. I heard shots and saw people falling in the battlefield. I felt scared and confused because it wasn't what I expected. I got out of there fast as I could but I heard it got to smelling like dead bodies.

A Letter Home
By Kelley Wesolowski

Private J. R. Montgomery who was mortally wounded wrote this letter to his father. The letter was stained with blood, it said:

Dear Father,
This is my letter to you ... I have been struck with a piece of shell and my right shoulder is horribly mangled and I know death is inevitable ... I know death is near, that I will die far from home and friends of my early youth, but I have friends here too who are kind to me. My friend Fairfax will write you at my request and give you the particulars of my death. My grave will be marked 58 that you may visit if you desire so .... give my love to all my friends .... my strength fails me .... may we meet in heaven.
Your dying son,

J. R. Montgomery

* * * *

The Bloodiest Day of the Civil War
By Tony Wesolowski

General Lee was planning to invade the North by dividing into four groups to take control of a Northern stronghold at Harper's Ferry. Lee's instructions to his troops were called "Special Orders 191". He sent orders to nine Generals. One of the Generals lost his orders. Two soldiers for the North found three cigars with a piece of paper wrapped around them. They said, "This is just our lucky day." Right before one of the soldiers lighted a cigar he saw in the corner of his eye the paper with the South's plans on it. He took the paper to his officer and that officer took the orders to General McClellan. He thought it might be a trick so he didn't go to the places on the paper. McClellan was so slow in acting that a man went and told General Lee to get his troops back together because the North knew their plans and they didn't want to die.

Later a battle did take place and it was the bloodiest one day battle of the war so far. One soldier leaning on a fence had over 57 bullet holes in him. It looked like a Gatlin gun shot him. There were so many dead soldiers that one man said, "You couldn't walk across the cornfield without stepping on dead soldiers."

If General McClellan wasn't so slow, the North could have wiped out the South in a heartbeat and the war would have been over.

* * * *

General McClellan
By Matt Loizeaux

In February 1862 Lincoln sent General George B. McClellan to march on Richmond. McClellan positioned his forces between the James and York rivers, at the tip of the peninsula. When he got close he stopped and waited while Lee and his troops were reinforced by "Stonewall" Jackson and they attacked the Union and drove them back to the tip of the peninsula.

This is the letter Lincoln later wrote, but did not send:

"My dear McClellan: If you don't want to use it *(the army)*, I should like to borrow it for a while.

Yours respectfully,

A. Lincoln"

* * * *

Alabama Farmer Disabled
By Bethany Powell

A Descendent of Private William Jefferson Parish

Private William Jefferson Parish of Company G, 15th Alabama Infantry Regiment as been permanently disabled by a fractured thigh after being severely injured at Chickamauga on September 20, 1863. Prior to this he was severely wounded at Cross Key, Virginia on June 8, 1862. Private Parish was born in Alabama and lives in Abbeville. He was 19 when he enlisted in Alabama, unmarried and a farmer. As you can see he was a very brave and dedicated Confederate soldier.

* * * *

The Battle of Antietam Creek
Contributed by Christina White

Taken from A Civil War Treasury of Tales, Legends and Folklore. Botkin, B.A.
New York: Promontory Press

*I thought a boy who shot me
    had a familiar face,
But in the battle's fury,
    'twas difficult to trace ....
Oh, I quickly ran unto him
    and heard his story o'er;
It was my long lost brother
    who lay welterin in his gore.*

OBITUARY

Daniel Tarbox
1844 - 1862

Daniel Tarbox, 18, of Brooklyn, Connecticut was wounded at Antietam, Maryland under General Burnside on September 17. He died on September 18 at the age of eighteen years and four months.

He is survived by his mother and father, Daniel and Lucelia Tarbox, as well as four sisters and two brothers.

As Reported By Richard Barnard,
A Descendent of Daniel Tarbox

A PRISONER
By Reporter: Megan Purvis

The prison cells aren't fit for humans. Dirt and filth line the cells. There are thirty men to a cell. The guards are callous and cruel. The inmates have not eaten since yesterday, because they are fed only once a day. Fights break out at all hours of the night, for lack of some way to occupy their time. A stale piece of cornbread, and a drink of unclean water, from a shared cup, is all that is received. Diseases are easily spread in such close quarters. Moans fill the night from the sick and dying. The jail smells of unbathed men. The scampering of rats fill the night with eerie sounds. The beds, a sleeping mat is shared with lice, fleas, and roaches. There is but a flicker of hope in the lives of those who have risked their lives for the sake of their country, and received nothing for their bravery.

* * * *

Sally Tompkins
By Marie Loizeaux

Sally Louisa Tompkins was born in Matthews County, Virginia. Sally Tompkins was a founder and supervisor in one of the best-run hospitals in Richmond. They moved to Richmond at the death of Sally's father. Sally Tompkins was the only woman holding a commission in the Confederate Army. She also had a very wealthy family. She was about five feet tall. She had dignity, a strong mind, determination, and unusual physical endurance. All the soldiers in the hospital called her "the little lady with the milk white hands." Most of the soldiers wanted to marry her but she says she'll never marry...

* * * *

An Old Man Fights
By Tony Wesolowski

There was a battle in Gettysburg. The Rebel soldiers ran off all the cows so John Burns got his flintlock and joined in the fight. He was the only citizen that fought in this battle. John Burns was 70 years old at the time.

Surprised By A Rebel At Gettysburg
By Kelley Wesolowski

Shooting hadn't stopped all morning and this battle was getting pretty intense. There hadn't even been a break of firing until around 11 o'clock. We were all very surprised when a Rebel sharpshooter shouted "Don't fire yanks!" and climbed out of a tree about 90 feet from us. Everybody looked on in curiosity. Several aimed at him but others checked him to see what would follow. He had a canteen in his hand and when he almost got to us we saw him kneel down and give a drink to one of our wounded who lay beyond us. We all cheered the Rebel and someone shouted, "Bully for you Johnny!". While all this was happening everybody had risen to their feet. As soon as the Rebel was done, he walked back, got in the tree and yelled, "Down Yanks! We're going to fire!" So we all got down and the firing resumed. I shall never forget this experience.

* * * *

A Kind Word From Lee
By Richard Barnard

After the Battle of Gettysburg, General Lee was riding through the field in retreat. Laying in the field was a Northern Federal soldier with his left leg shattered. As soon as the soldier recognized Lee he looked at him and shouted, "Hurrah for the Union!"

The General heard him, stopped his horse, walked toward him, bent down and said, "My son, I hope you will soon be well."

At these words the soldier was shocked! After all, Lee was on the opposite side. He had also just lost the battle and probably all his hopes. These words for a soldier who had only just finished taunting Lee. Realizing the true character of Lee the soldier cried himself to sleep that night on the battlefield.

Lee Asks Grant for Horses

By David Wesolowski

In April of 1965 General Grant and General Lee met together so Lee could surrender the army of Northern Virginia. Only officers were allowed to keep their sidearms but all men were allowed to return home undisturbed.

General Lee was bothered because his men were not allowed to keep their horses. He asked Grant, "Could my men please keep their horses because they own them and they need them to farm?" General Grant thought about it a while and then said, "Okay, I will arrange for that."

As Lee rode away, the soldiers wept, cursed or stared off into space. They couldn't believe their army had at long last surrendered.

Lee Accused of Treason
By Tony Wesolowski

General Lee was accused of treason by a district court judge from the north. On July 13, 1865, he wrote a letter to President Andrew Johnson asking to be pardoned. He sent the letter to General Grant and asked him to endorse the request. General Grant sent the request to President Johnson along with his endorsement.

Lee was never brought to trial but he was not pardoned until long after his death.

It Ends Where It Begins
By Stacey Wesolowski

Four years ago the first battle of the Civil War started on property owned by Major McLean. After the fighting started Major McLean moved to some other property of his in Appomattox, Virginia. Much to his surprise, Lee's army last fought in Appomattox and Lee decided to surrender to Grant in McLean's parlor. After the surrender Major McLean said, "The war began in my front yard and ended in my parlor." On that same day Federal officers stripped Major McLean's home for souvenirs.

Lincoln Assassinated!
By Marie N. Loizeaux

President Lincoln was making great plans to unite the North with the South. Unfortunately he never lived long enough to carry out his plans. About a week ago, President Lincoln was assassinated. This is how it happened. President Lincoln was taking his wife to a play at Ford's theater in Washington D.C. A half-crazed actor named John Wilkes Booth got through the theater to where the President was sitting, pulled out a gun and shot him in the head. Some men carried him to a house across the street from the theater, where he died the next morning a little after seven o'clock.

The above device, used by the Confederates to produce coded messages, has been confiscated by Northern troops.

NOTE: *This newsletter is comprised of articles taken from the eight newsletters that were written by the children (ages 9 - 15) who participated in our Civil War Unit Study.*

Summary of Major Battles
Chapter 3

    Keeping a chart filled out during the unit study will enable the student to remember the "who, what, when and where" information they are gaining. The sample chart which is included at the end of this chapter covers the firing upon Fort Sumter, seven major battles, and Lee's surrender at Appomattox. Feel free to add to or subtract from this chart as you wish. You may decide to study a battle which took place closer to your home town in lieu of one of those listed. Or you may wish to extend the study and cover many more battles than those included in this chapter. For your convenience, a short summary of each battle selected for this study, as well as the surrender, is included. Researching other battles is easy to do if you have access to a public library. It can be very stimulating and rewarding as well. One of the most helpful books I found is entitled, *The Civil War Dictionary, Revised Edition* (Boatner III, Mark M., New York: Random House, Inc., 1987). It cites nearly every famous person, place, and event which occurred during the war.

    The events included in this chapter are as follows:

The Firing Upon Fort Sumter -------------------------- **Page 18**

The Battle of Bull Run - Manassas Junction ------------- **Page 20**

The Monitor - Virginia (Merrimac) Duel ---------------- **Page 21**

The Shiloh Campaign ------------------------------- **Page 23**

The Second Battle of Bull Run ---------------------- **Page 25**

Antietam - Sharpsburg Battle ----------------------- **Page 27**

The Vicksburg Campaign --------------------------- **Page 29**

The Battle of Gettysburg -------------------------- **Page 32**

The Surrender at Appomattox ----------------------- **Page 38**

The Chart -------------------------------------- **Page 41**

The Firing Upon Fort Sumter

When: April 1861
Where: South Carolina
Officers: North - Anderson
          South - Beauregard
Results: Southern victory
Casualties: North - 1 killed, 2 wounded

When first visiting Charleston, South Carolina, in 1991 with my sister-in-law, I had no idea of the large part that this city played in the Civil War. What a great place to visit! The restored homes are beautiful and the choice of fine restaurants is overwhelming (if you do get to visit this city, try the seafood casserole served at "Aw Shucks" - it's indescribably delicious).

Although I didn't visit the fort in 1991, I did learn a little war history as I visited a plantation on the outskirts of Charleston. It was proclaimed to be the only estate that was not burned by Sherman on his march to the sea. The lady of the home slaughtered all of her cattle in the yard, left them to rot, and then ran a disease flag up on the premises. By the time the Northern Army arrived, the stench was so bad that they stayed as far away from the home as possible. The house has been kept in its original state as much as possible. The children's heights, marked by pencil on the door jambs, remain there today. The name of this plantation is the Drayton Plantation. Be sure to take the time to visit this historic landmark if you are in the vicinity.

Our family visited Fort Sumter in August of 1995. We were forewarned by Bob Farewell not to take the last boat of the day over to the island because our time would be too short to see everything. We were distraught to learn that the only boat going over when we arrived in the city was the last boat of the day. Bob was right — we felt rushed, but it was a great experience.

Fort Sumter is built upon a man-made island just outside Charleston, South Carolina, in the middle of its main shipping channels. Shortly after Lincoln was elected in 1860, South Carolina was the first

Battle Summaries — Chapter 3

state to secede on December 20, 1860. Six days later, on December 26, Major Robert Anderson (Southern born but in command of the Northern forts in Charlestown harbor) secretly withdrew his troops from Fort Moultrie and placed them in Fort Sumter. The Southerners constructed batteries on Morris Island and blocked boats trying to send supplies and reinforcements to Fort Sumter. On April 10, 1861, Beauregard (now in command of the Southerners) demanded the evacuation of Fort Sumter. Anderson replied that he would evacuate by the 15th unless he received further instructions. Beauregard notified Anderson that he would open fire on the morning of the 12th, and he did so at 4:30 a.m. The construction of the fort was incomplete, and the Northerners were at a disadvantage without full protection. They were encouraged by the sight of reinforcement ships arriving, but these were blocked and could not reach the fort.

In addition to creating serious damage, the Southerners noticed that their hot shot had been successful in setting several buildings on fire within the fort. Because of this, they increased that type of firing the following day, and by noon the fires were raging, endangering the lives of all those remaining on the island. Anderson surrendered with the honors of war. When I first learned about this, I read that there were no fatalities, and only a dog was killed. Later I read that there was indeed a fatality, which sadly enough occurred during the surrender. The Southerners graciously allowed the Northerners a 100-gun salute, but on the 50th round an explosion took place and a Private Hough became the first Northern soldier of the war to be killed. Another man died later from wounds incurred by the explosion and still another was seriously injured.

Ironically, on April 14, 1865 — just a few hours before Lincoln's assassination — Anderson was present when the original flag was again raised over Fort Sumter.

Interesting Assignments

*What was the personal relationship between
Beauregard and Anderson?*

*Which Southern officer was responsible
for giving the order to fire upon the Fort?*

The Battle of Bull Run - Manassas Junction

When: July 1861
Where: Virginia
Officers: North - McDowell
            South - Beauregard
Results: Southern victory
Casualties: North - 418 killed, 1,011 wounded, 1,216 missing
            South - 387 killed, 1,582 wounded, 12 missing

You are probably wondering why some battles are known by two names. I was curious about this as well, but instead of telling you the reason, I'll let it remain a mystery for your students to solve.

If it were not such a serious matter with lives being lost and its accompanying hardships, many aspects of this battle would be comical. For instance, a Southern troop marching into the area discovered a creek which had to be crossed. Not wanting to risk falling off a log and wetting their shoes and socks, the soldiers began removing their footwear. Can you picture hundreds of men, prior to the rigors of battle, seated on an embankment in order to carefully remove their shoes and socks? When their officer arrived to see what was holding things up, he realized that his soldiers were afraid of falling into water which was only "ankle deep." He made them all put their shoes and socks back on and wade right through the creek!

Many of the Washington society folks thought the battle would be an interesting place for a picnic. They assumed that the Southern army would be easily routed and that they would enjoy watching. What they did not count on was the disorganization of both sides, the strength of the Southern army, the fear caused by the "Rebel Yell," and the Northern troops running from battle right through the picnic area, wreaking havoc on everyone's afternoon plans.

Stonewall Jackson received his nickname during this battle. Although he was on the side of the Southerners, his sister Laura was a Northern sympathizer She sent a message by a Northern soldier stating that she could "take care of the wounded Federals as fast as Thomas would wound them."

The statistics show that the Northerners actually fought more effectively than the Southerners. The reason that the South won this battle is because both sides were inexperienced and the advantage typically goes to the defender. Many soon realized that this war was not going to come to an end as quickly as had been assumed.

* Interesting assignments *

How did "Stonewall" Jackson receive his nickname?

Why did Major Wilmer McLean say, "The war began in my front yard and ended in my parlor"?

The *Monitor-Virginia* (*Merrimac*) Duel

When: March 9, 1862
Where: Hampton Roads, Virginia
Officers: North - Worden
            South - Jones
Results: Northern withdrawal, Southern victory
Casualties: North - 409 deaths
            South - 2 deaths, 9 wounded

This battle turned the tide in naval strategy and is well worth studying because of that fact. The North's *Monitor* and the South's *Virginia* were ships that both made naval history because they were the first "ironclads" ever involved in war.

The *Virginia* was actually a raised Northern ship (the *Merrimac*) that was "an ingenious adaptation of the materials at hand and a tribute to her builders' skill at improvision" (Potter, E. B., *The United States and World Sea Power*, Englewood Cliffs, N.J.: Prentice-Hall, Inc., 1955.) The *Virginia* was covered with crisscrossed four inch wrought-iron bars. The boat gave the appearance of a floating barn roof.

The *Monitor*, on the other hand, was a completely new design that had been developing in the mind of John Ericsson for many years. It has been estimated that this ship contained at least 40 patentable ideas. The circular turret was covered by eight layers of one-inch iron plates, and the sides of the deck had four-and-a-half inches of iron armor. It had two nicknames: "Ericsson's Folly" and "The Yankee Cheese Box on a Raft."

On Saturday, March 8, the *Virginia* rammed the *Cumberland*, a 30-gun frigate, and shelled the 50-gun *Congress*. The *Cumberland* sank with the *Virginia's* ram imbedded in her side. The *Congress* surrendered after being forced aground.

On Sunday morning, March 9, the *Virginia* opened the battle with the *Monitor,* and the ironclads actually touched several times during this battle. The *Virginia* was difficult to maneuver while the *Monitor* maneuvered well. The duel was indecisive until the *Monitor* was forced to withdraw because of a hit on the sight hole of the pilot house. Jones, on the *Virginia*, ceased fire when he was unable to do any further damage. His ship was badly damaged. The prow was lost during the ramming of the *Cumberland*. Jones returned the boat to Norfolk and it remained there for repairs for almost a month.

* Interesting assignments *

What ultimately became of these two ships?

Why is the <u>Merrimac</u> spelled without a "k" in some instances, and with a "k" at other times?

The Shiloh Campaign

When: April, 1862
Where: Tennessee
Officers: North - Grant, Wallace, Sherman and Buell
South - Johnston and Beauregard
Results: Both sides claim victory
Casualties: North - 1,754 killed, 8,408 wounded, 2,885 missing
South - 1,723 killed, 8,012 wounded, 959 missing

"The Battle of Blunders" is what many call this campaign. It's interesting to read the differing reports that came from both sides involved in the Battle of Shiloh. There are some historians who feel that Generals Grant, Sherman (North) and Beauregard (South) should have been court-martialled and held responsible for the large blood bath that needlessly took place at Shiloh. These same people feel that had General Johnston not been killed, he too should have been court-martialled.

According to first-hand reports, this battle was full of mistakes, commands that were too general, and orders that were blatantly disobeyed. Neither the Northerners or the Southerners saw the obvious need for securing Crump's Landing. The Northerners had control of this landing mainly because of the stragglers hanging out there. The Southerners thought the Northerners had charge of the landing because someone erroneously reported that the stragglers were in fact reinforcements. Had the Southerners been able to take control of this landing, they could then have prevented the arrival of Northern reinforcements and then could have won this battle.

General Grant separated his troops with a swamp in between. His headquarters was located nine miles away — <u>downstream</u>! He mistakenly supposed that the South would not attack and that he could fight an offensive battle when Buell's reinforcements arrived.

Field officers for the North realized that the South was planning to attack and sent such a message to General Sherman. But, as late as <u>the night before</u> the South attacked, Sherman sent Grant a message that there was <u>no danger</u> of an immediate enemy attack.

Generals Johnston and Beauregard were not even in sync with

their plans. Johnston's orders were so broad that when he was killed in battle, his troops were not sure how to proceed. Beauregard either blatantly disregarded Johnston's command or just came up with a different plan which he thought was superior. He planned a full frontal attack but didn't really have the resources to carry it out.

General Buell and his reinforcements arrived days before the Southerns expected them. Why they didn't send scouts to discover this information is unknown. These reinforcements arrived by way of Crump's Landing, enabling the North to complete this battle by overtaking the South. The South retreated but General Grant did not pursue the retreating soldiers. He felt that his boys were too tired to fight any further.

Boatner says (*The Civil War Dictionary*),

> *Although both sides claimed the victory, it was a Northern victory, since it forced the enemy back on Corinth, forced them to evacuate much of Tennessee, and opened the way to the final splitting of the Southerners along the Mississippi. The Southerners failed to destroy the Northern army and were forced to withdraw from the battlefield, leaving many of their dead and wounded. The generalship on both sides was defective; 'Bloody Shiloh' was a 'Soldier's Battle.'*

* Interesting assignments *

What did CSA (Confederate States of America) President Jefferson Davis say about General Albert S. Johnston?

What had Grant done prior to his service in the Civil War that brought him and his family shame?

Research the numbers actually involved in this campaign. There is some disagreement about the total number of troops involved, but most agree the Northerners far outnumbered the Southerners.

The Second Battle of Bull Run

When: August 29-30, 1862
Where: Virginia
Officers: North - Pope, McClellan
             South - Lee, Jackson, Longstreet and Hill
Results: Southern victory
Casualties: North - 1,724 killed, 8,372 wounded, 5,958 missing
             South - 1,481 killed, 7,627 wounded, 89 missing

John Pope was the officer in charge of the Northern troops during this campaign. It is said that Lincoln's selection of Pope is one of the errors he made during the war. Being a "western man," Pope was not very well liked by his forces in the east. Even the mild-mannered Lee took a personal disliking to this enemy, saying he must be suppressed. Jackson and Longstreet had their chance to destroy Pope's army during this battle, but tactical failures prohibited this. Although far outnumbered by the Northerners, the Southerners maintained the offensive, and Lee's over-all strategic accomplishments were remarkable.

One of the tactical errors made by Jackson was caused by his "mania for secrecy." Because he did not keep his division commanders informed of his plans, his troops movements were slowed down. During one skirmish, the Southern calvary captured Pope's headquarters and brought back news that Northern reinforcements would soon enlarge Pope's ranks to 130,000 men. After receiving this information, Lee developed a plan that is still controversial among historians today. Facing an army almost twice the size of his, Lee planned to split his troops and surprise the enemy. His plan depended on speed, deception and the skill of his subordinate commanders. Lee knew that his only other alternative was a defensive battle which would have led to defeat.

Taking advantage of the slow Northern reaction and the panic which he knew would ensue from his plan, Lee proceeded. Pope was aware of Jackson's movements but did not pursue him. When Pope learned there were enemy forces to his rear, he was convinced that this was more than just a raid, so he started withdrawing. He ordered a concentration of troops at Gainesville, Warrenton Junction, and in between. At this point Pope could have blocked Longstreet and wiped out Jackson, but Jackson's moves so thoroughly confused Pope that he let this chance slip by. Pope finally ordered his troops to go after Jackson, but not before Longstreet joined Jackson. The Battle of Groveton took place on August 28, 1862. Casualties were high, both Southern division commanders were wounded, and the Northerners did not withdraw until around midnight. This set the stage for the Second Battle of Bull Run.

Pope could have destroyed Jackson's troops the first day before he was joined by Longstreet, but his piece-meal frontal attacks failed to drive Jackson from his strong position. Longstreet joined Jackson. Had Longstreet attacked on the first day of the battle, he would have insured a victory for Lee which would have destroyed the majority of the Northern army.

On the second day, Pope still was not aware that Longstreet had joined Jackson, and he suffered a decisive tactical defeat. Lee was successful in driving the Northern army back into Washington.

* Interesting assignments *

What position was offered to Lee by the Northerners before he accepted the command of the Army of Northern Virginia?

What was so offensive about Pope's published address?

Johnny and Danielle Ballentine

Antietam - Sharpsburg Battle

When: September, 1862
Where: Maryland
Officers: North - McClellan
South - Lee
Results: Northern victory
Casualties: North - 2,108 killed, 9,549 wounded, 753 missing
South - 2,700 killed, 9,024 wounded, 2,000 missing

Known as the bloodiest single day of the war, this battle is considered by many to be the turning point of the war. Historians believe that the Battle of Antietam not only set the stage for Lincoln to announce the Emancipation Proclamation, but that the sentiment in Europe switched from the side of the South to the side of the North, thereby destroying the South's last hope for foreign assistance.

Until now all the battles had taken place on Southern soil. Lee planned to take his army through Maryland and into Pennsylvania where he hoped to destroy important bridges and railroads. Lee's plans for this battle were brilliant, but the outcome was altered considerably by an unfortunate discovery. Lee's strategy was to capture Harper's Ferry in Maryland, a Northern stronghold where 12,000 soldiers were stationed. Lee decided that the best way to accomplish this was to split up his army temporarily. His generals argued with him against this decision, thinking their armies would be too vulnerable and easily defeated if divided. Lee knew this was a possibility, but having fought General George McClellan before, he knew how cautious and slow McClellan was. Lee felt confident that by the time General McClellan took action, he could have his troops back together as one army. Lee called in one of his colonels and dictated "Special Orders 191" to be distributed to his nine commanding officers.

Washington found out that Lee was in Maryland, and Lincoln ordered McClellan to pursue and destroy the Southern army as quickly as possible. McClellan set out in search of Lee but was unsure of his location and which way he was headed. Four days after leaving Washington, a group of Northern soldiers set up camp outside of

Frederick, Maryland. A few days prior, this had been a camp for the Southern soldiers, and they left litter on the ground. A Corporal Mitchell and Sergeant Bliss unpacked and sat down under a tree to rest. Mitchell saw something that caught his eye on the ground and he picked it up. Much to his delight, he found three cigars wrapped in paper. Giving a cigar to Bliss, Mitchell started to throw the paper away when something written on it caught his eye. It was Lee's "Special Orders 191." It was passed from hand to hand until it was given to General McClellan. He was ecstatic. Until now, he was not even sure where Lee was; now he had complete details of his planned attack. He telegraphed Lincoln and told him, "I have all the plans of the rebels, and will catch them in their own trap."

Had McClellan rushed to where he now knew Lee's army was, the war may well have ended with this battle. Due to his cautious nature, and because some of his advisors warned him that this may be a trap set by Lee, McClellan hesitated for 16 hours. Meanwhile, a businessman who was present when McClellan was presented the special orders made his way to the Southern lines. He told a Southern officer about this piece of paper and McClellans reaction to it. Lee concluded that McClellan knew something about his plans and decided he would need to stop and take a stand. He picked Antietam Creek, near Sharpsburg.

McClellan continued his slow approach toward Lee, yet when he finally reached Antietam Creek, he let another day go by. Meanwhile, more troops were able to join Lee. On September 17, <u>FOUR</u> days after McClellan had received a copy of Lee's plans, the battle began. The Southern army was tired, hungry and shoeless, but fought with determination. The Northern soldiers were led by officers who were not as experienced as the Southern officers, but they charged again and again. Each side stood its ground. On one forty acre field every single stalk of corn was cut down. The dead bodies were so numerous that a survivor reported that he could have walked across the field on the bodies of the dead. A soldier found slumped over a fence post had over 57 bullets in his body. One section of the battlefield was called "Bloody Lane." Over 23,000 lay dead or wounded after one day of battle.

Lee did not withdraw immediately the next day, but around noon Jackson and Longstreet convinced him that a counterattack was impossible, and he returned his army to Virginia. McClellan, despite the fact that 24,000 of his troops were not even involved in the battle, and 12,000 fresh troops arrived on the morning of the 18th, decided that his army was too badly crippled to renew the attack.

* Interesting assignments *

Consider all the "what ifs" involved in this battle.

Why did the sentiment in Europe swing to the side of the North after this battle?

Which officer do some historians think is responsible for losing his "Special Orders 191"?

What do you think about McClellan being so slow and cautious?

The Vicksburg Campaign

When: April - July, 1863
Where: Mississippi
Officers: North - Grant
South - Pemberton
Results: Northern victory
Casualties: North - 410 killed, 1,844 wounded, 187 missing
South - 381 killed, 1,800 wounded, 1,670 missing

Historians say Ulysses S. Grant achieved one of the most brilliant military successes in history with the fall of Vicksburg. The surrender by the South took place just one day after the Northern victory at Gettysburg, sealing the fate of the Southern cause. Not only was the South cut in half, but of greater importance was the fact that the Mississippi River was now open for trade between the Midwest and the outside world.

This campaign actually began in October of 1862, with Grant's capture of several forts down the Mississippi. On October 25, 1862, Grant was given the command of the Department of the Tennessee. Admiral Farragut had captured New Orleans for the North and secured the river as far north as Baton Rouge.

One of the major battles of this campaign was the battle for Champion's Hill on May 16, 1863. Pemberton had been ordered to strike the rear flank of Grant's army, but he did nothing until May 15. Then he moved within striking distance of Grant but changed his mind and decided to unite instead with Johnston at Brownsville. Champion's Hill is about 75 feet high and provides a good position for blocking the roads to Vicksburg from the East. Pemberton gathered approximately 22,000 men to oppose McPherson and McClernands' 29,000. Instead of attacking the south flank of the Southern army as soon as he made contact, McClernand waited four-and-a-half hours for orders; when he did finally attack, it was without vigor. Historians say he forfeited an opportunity to destroy this entire army by his lack of aggressiveness. The hill changed hands several times during the fighting. Pemberton blamed General Loring for the Southern failure because he failed to obey Pemberton's orders to first attack McClernand on the south flank and then move to support the defense of the north flank. Pemberton retreated.

Pemberton's forces did manage to slow Grant's pursuit somewhat by destroying bridges. Grant crossed the river on pontoon bridges on May 18. On May 19, Grant ordered an assault on Vicksburg. Pemberton's forces repulsed this attack all along the line. Grant ordered another attack on May 22. This was to be a frontal assault. He planned this skirmish to be won before Johnston could gather his forces and come to Pemberton's aid. He underestimated the strength of the Southern army and its will to resist. After heavy fighting, Grant's attacks were repulsed. He was ready to call a halt to the attack but did not do so because of misleading reports of success delivered to him by McClernand. He ordered a final assault. Grant later admitted that he regretted ordering this attack as Pemberton's 18,000 troops stopped 45,000 Northern infantry, inflicting 3,200 casualties.

Grant made no further attempt to take the city by assault, but decided to starve the Southerners into surrender. Several attempts were made to penetrate the Southern defense by the ancient technique of mining. Three times the North planned to explode mines as a means of piercing the Southern fortifications. Pemberton's situation became more hopeless as time went by due to the constant shelling and the growing shortage of rations. Almost 50 percent (10,000) of his troops were unfit for battle due to wounds and illness. The civilians were suffering as well from the unceasing bombardment and the shortage of food. On July 3, Grant and Pemberton met to discuss terms for surrender. Pemberton agreed to surrender on July 4, thinking that since it was Independence Day, Grant would show his troops some compassion. At the time Pemberton was criticized for agreeing to this date, and some were even suspicious of treachery on his part. Grant demanded unconditional surrender, but he was criticized as well for giving parole to Pemberton's force. Grant's reasoning for this was to avoid the loss of time and transportation necessary to evacuate such a large number of prisoners of war.

* Interesting assignments *

What is the nickname given to General Grant that has the same abbreviation as his name (U.S.)?

There were at least five unsuccessful attempts against Vicksburg before Grant's victory - what were they?

What part did Northern Admiral David Farragut play in this campaign?

Loizeaux Family Portrait

The Battle of Gettysburg

When: July 1 - 3, 1863
Where: Pennsylvania
Officers: North - Meade
            South - Lee
Results: Northern victory
Casualties: North - 3,155 killed, 14,529 wounded, 5,365 missing
            South - 3,903 killed, 18,735 wounded, 5,425 missing

Writing a summary of this battle is a monumental task. There have been many books dedicated to the Battle of Gettysburg alone. I read several of these books, including *Killer Angels*, the book on which the movie *Gettysburg* is based (Bob Farewell, author of the foreword, played a small part in this movie), and had very mixed emotions about where to place the fault for this bloodbath. Some historians seem to believe that General Lee wasn't thinking clearly due to the recent loss of Stonewall Jackson, and therefore issued impossible orders. I tend to believe that although General Lee did feel a great loss at Jackson's death, his plans may have worked had his commanders carried out his orders fully and expeditiously.

On June 27, General Hooker (Northern army) asked to be relieved of his command because he wanted Lincoln to give him full authority to make decisions, and Lincoln refused. Lincoln accepted his resignation and switched the command of the Northern army from Hooker to Meade. The timing for this change wasn't the best, but many senior officers had lost confidence in Hooker after his failure at Chancellorsville. Meade never backed away from a fight, and he now had troops that were more seasoned than before.

General Lee decided to take his army north for several reasons. The farmlands in Pennsylvania were untouched from the war; consequently, there would be plenty of supplies of meat and grain. Lee knew that moving north would confuse the enemy, causing them to assume that he was going to attack Washington. The enemy would then fall back to defend the capital. Until this time all of the Northern generals had been conservative and predictable fighters, preferring to defend rather than attack. At this point Hooker was in charge, and Lee knew this was true of his leadership as well. Lee didn't care about attacking Washington. He wanted to go further north to threaten Philadelphia and Baltimore and cut Washington off from the rest of the country. The war might not have been won outright with this battle plan, but it would have certainly put pressure on Lincoln to negotiate peace in the South's favor. Lee also was hoping to draw the enemy out into the open to fight at a battlefield of Lee's choice. Lieutenant General James Longstreet, one of Lee's most trusted commanders, did not like this plan. He voiced his opposition from the beginning and tried to persuade others to side with him. Lee listened to Longstreet's arguments, but felt that it was best to continue as planned.

On June 25, Lee sent Major General James E. B. "Jeb" Stuart and his cavalry off on an important mission. They were to locate the Northern army and report its whereabouts and size as soon as possible — within a few days. Lee also wanted Stuart to harass and distract the Northern army so that Lee could get his troops into Pennsylvania. Here is another area where historians' accounts differ. It is said that Stuart overdid his job because of his insistence that his men travel completely around the Northern army, returning to Lee so late that his information was not only useless, but that his actions were to blame for this battle's outcome. He did not return to Lee's camp until July 2 — the second day of the battle. Lee was at a huge disadvantage at this point because he had not received the information he requested of Stuart. This led him to a wrong conclusion that the main enemy line was along the Emmitsburg Pike, with its flank near the Wheat Field. Lee planned for Longstreet to attack this flank and then attack along the pike. Lee's plan was defective due to inadequate information, but it was made worse by his commander's reluctance to attack on the North. For these reasons, Lee decided to reduce the overextension of his army. According to Stuart, he was trying to get back to Lee, but because of the huge size of the Northern army, his paths were blocked and he had to go further out of his way before he could return.

On June 30, the Northern army realized that the Southern army was in Gettysburg and would more than likely attack the next day. Buford (Northern general) sent a small force to occupy the town of Gettysburg and ordered the rest of his men to take positions on the ridge near the Seminary. Buford held the best position and for this reason was able to beat back the initial charge of the Southern army. As usual, the Southern army was not about to give up. They moved their artillery and started a second advance, inching their way closer and closer to Buford's men. It was at this point that Reynolds arrived to reinforce Buford. Reynolds sent five thousand men into the fight and ordered the rest to the city of Gettysburg. Among Reynolds' troops were the seasoned and tenacious fighters known as the Iron Brigade. Reynolds wrote the following message to Buford: "I will fight him inch by inch, and if driven into town I will barricade the streets and hold him back as long as possible." Fifteen minutes later a Southern sharpshooter shot Reynolds and he died.

Fighting was so close on the ridge that the men were using their bayonets and the butts of their rifles to defend themselves. Neither side backed off, and by noon the Iron Brigade had been shattered. Another five thousand Southerners arrived, and this overwhelmed the Northern army. They began to retreat to the hills where their artillery was stationed so they could regroup. Lee arrived and took stock of the situation. Only half of his army had arrived at this point, and Stuart had not returned, so he still did not know the location of the remaining Northern army. For this reason Lee did not have the confidence to order a full attack. Had he attacked with the full Northern army arrayed for battle, Lee would have risked total annihilation of his men. Not knowing his posture at this point, he ordered his men to pull back for the night. Meanwhile, Meade arrived and conferred with his officers. He knew that to retreat would admit defeat and allow the possibility of an attack upon Washington or Baltimore. The Northern army was now at an advantage because they not only had a good secure position in the hills, but by dawn they would have 75,000 more troops in the area. Retreat was out of the question. This was the end of the first day of the Battle of Gettysburg.

Firing had begun as early as 4:00 a.m. on July 2. The Northern soldiers were positioned on Cemetery Ridge and had a view of the valley for miles. Lee's plan was to attack both flanks of the Northern battle line in order to push them off the high ground. Longstreet again argued against this plan and suggested they strike Meade from the rear. Stuart still had not arrived. Lee still did not know the whereabouts of the rest of the Northern army, and was opposed to sending in troops to an area that may open his troops up to an ambush. Lee said, "The enemy is there and I am going to fight him there." It took until mid-afternoon for Longstreet to position his men. Some feel that he was intentionally dragging his feet because he objected to Lee's plans. Once he attacked, he did so with full force. The Southern army was gaining an upper hand until Major General G. K. Warrent saw a line of Southerners approaching Little Round Top. He immediately ordered a brigade to the top of the hill and left them to secure artillery. He was able to get everything into place on top of the hill in time to hold off the Southern soldiers. Luck and timing seemed to be on Meade's side. The Southern troops were trying over and over to storm Culp's Hill but were driven off with each attempt. Late in the afternoon Meade sent in a fresh brigade and pushed back the Southern army. Lee had failed to destroy either of the North's flanks. Meade conferred with his officers to determine their stand. Knowing that they had the superior position, they decided to continue the battle. The discussion in Lee's tent was very heated. Pickett had arrived with reinforcements, and Stuart had returned to camp. Lee wanted to attack the center of the North's position but Longstreet, once again, was opposed to this plan. Longstreet wanted to withdraw and find better fighting grounds. Lee felt they had come too close to withdraw now and with the arrival of both Stuart and Pickett the Southern army should be able to push the Northern army back. This was the end of day two of the Battle of Gettysburg.

Fighting began early on July 3. Lee again met with Longstreet and Pickett to go over the details of the charge one more time. Longstreet tried <u>again</u> to talk Lee out of the uphill fight. Lee was convinced that the Northern soldiers would panic in the heat of the battle, and that the South would win. Longstreet was so opposed to this charge that he delegated the actual duty of giving the order to the officer directing the Southern artillery fire. After this, Longstreet became quiet and seemed reluctant to issue any orders. At ten minutes to one o'clock, the cannon fire from the Southern line began. The plan was for the cannons to continue firing in order to secure protection for the charging army.

The cannonade continued until half past two o'clock. At this point the Southern general in charge of the artillery sent a message to Pickett that his artillery would soon run out and that if they were going to charge, they should do so immediately. Here is another area where historians disagree with details of the events. Some say that Pickett was waiting for the actual order to come from Longstreet (which Longstreet had supposedly delegated to the artillery general). Did Pickett not know this? Some say that Pickett and Longstreet waited so long before charging that their defeat was imminent. Others say that Lee's plans were exceedingly faulty, and that trying to charge a fortified enemy secured behind stone walls on a hill was sure defeat.

After receiving a second note from the artillery general ordering Pickett to charge, he rode over to Longstreet and asked if he should advance. An officer nearby described the scene as follows: "General L. read the note and . . . turned around in his saddle and would not answer. Pickett immediately saluted, and said: 'I am going to lead my division forward, sir' and galloped off to put it in motion; on which General L. left his staff and rode out alone." It was too late. The Southern artillery was too low to continue giving cannon coverage. The smoke (intended to provide covering) was clearing when the Southern army finally charged, <u>uncovered,</u> up the hill to fight the enemy. Within two hours the bloodbath was all but ended. The North repulsed the Southern army and the battlefield was covered with the dead and wounded. A mile away General Lee tried to encourage the retreating solders, saying, "It is all my fault. All this will come right in the end, but in the meantime, all good men must rally." Most of the soldiers took off their hats and cheered him. Some historians say Pickett placed all the blame on Lee and became very bitter toward him. This was the end of the three day Battle of Gettysburg.

General Lee awaited an attack on the fourth of July, but it began to rain and by evening it was storming. Lee began his retreat in weather which made pursuit most difficult. Lincoln, however, wanted Meade to pursue Lee and finish the destruction of Lee's army, thereby ending the war. Meade had no intention of charging Lee's army directly so he sent out cavalry to find Lee's position. He discovered that Lee was in a strong defensive position at the Potomac, so he postponed attacking. This upset Lincoln, who sent Meade a message not to let the enemy escape. Meade resented being told what to do. He sent Lincoln a message telling him that his army was short of rations and tired, but that he would use his utmost efforts to push the army forward. By morning most of Lee's army had crossed the Potomac by way of a hastily constructed bridge. This infuriated Lincoln, who responded, "I could have whipped Lee myself."

This battle, although it took place two years before the war actually ended, was a major turning point. The South lost one third of its army and would never regain its full fighting force or threaten the North again. After the North realized how badly the South had been beaten, they began to support Lincoln more fully, and in 1864 he was reelected to office.

There were so many dead bodies left on the battlefield that they were hurriedly buried in shallow, mass graves. The smell was unbearable. As farmers ploughed for a late season crop, they couldn't discern the location of the graves and consequently dug up bodies. The only real solution was to dig up all the bodies and give them a real burial. A local cemetery association wanted the families of the dead to pay for this. A Gettysburg resident, David Wills, heard about this and said that it wouldn't be fair. He felt that these soldiers had already paid the ultimate price for their country. Wills proposed that a National Soldiers Cemetery be established with the costs being shared by all the Northern states. The governor agreed and sixteen acres of battlefield land was purchased for $2,475.97. The work began in October and took over a year to complete. A formal dedication ceremony was planned for November 19, 1863, and this is when Lincoln delivered his famous "Gettysburg Address."

* Interesting assignments *

Who was asked to be the honored speaker at the Gettysburg dedication?

Who was John Burns and what part did he play in this battle?

Memorize the opening paragraph to "The Gettysburg Address."

What was the response of the press when Lincoln completed his speech?

Why isn't there a photograph of Lincoln delivering his speech at Gettysburg?

The Surrender at Appomattox

When: April 9, 1865
Where: Virginia
Officers: North - Grant
          South - Lee
Results: Beginning of the end

When I began studying the Civil War in earnest, I had assumed that the war was over upon Lee's surrender. Although it was the beginning of the end, Lee only surrendered his army of Northern Virginia. Soon afterwards, however, the other Southern armies followed suit.

Lee was planning to move south to join J. E. Johnston's forces which were retreating from North Carolina. Southern forces from Petersburg, Bermuda Hundred, and Richmond headed for a junction at Amelia Courthouse. They were to receive supplies there and board a train in order to meet Johnston. Grant's swift actions prohibited Lee's troops from receiving supplies and joining up with Johnston. Lee probably would not have surrendered at this time but the supplies were destroyed, a union with Johnston was halted, and a retreat was blocked. Lee's troops were hungry, tired and ill-equipped. Surrender was the only option. On April 9, 1865, Lee surrendered to Grant in the parlor of Major McLean's home in Appomattox. J. E. Johnston asked for an armistice on the 14th of April, and surrendered to Sherman on the 26th. Richard Taylor surrendered on May 4, thus ending the Southern resistance east of the Mississippi. E. Kirby Smith surrendered his Trans-Mississippi Department on May 26, 1865.

Around noon on Sunday, April 9, 1865, Major McLean was walking down the street when one of Lee's aides stopped him. He asked McLean if he knew of a place that would be appropriate for General Lee to meet with General Grant. McLean showed the officer an unoccupied brick building in the center of the village, but when he was shown the unfurnished interior, the officer asked if there might be another place more suitable. McLean took him to his own home and showed him his parlor. The aide approved, and Grant received Lee's surrender at this location. Lee asked that his men be able to keep their horses as they would need them when they returned home. Grant agreed to this condition.

By 4:00 p.m., it was all over and McLean's house was promptly looted for souveniers. McLean insisted that he did not want to sell anything. He was besieged by offers, many pressing money into his hands. General Sheridan bought the table on which the terms of the surrender were written. It is now located in the Smithsonian Institution. Some officers simply took the furnishings they requested after McLean's refusal to sell to them. Chairs were cut up and pieces sold as mementos. Upholstery was shredded.

The following quote is a description of Lincoln's reaction upon hearing the news of Lee's surrender:

On the day of the receipt of the news of the capitulation of Lee, the Cabinet meeting was held an hour earlier than usual. Neither the President nor any member was able, for a long time, to give utterance to his feelings. At the suggestion of Mr. Lincoln all dropped on their knees, and offered, in silence and in tears, their humble and heartfelt acknowledgments to the Almighty for the triumph He had granted to the national cause.

Lee wrote a "Farewell to the Army of Northern Virginia" as follows:

After four years of arduous service, marked by unsurpassed courage and fortitude, the Army of Northern Virginia has been compelled to yield to overwhelming numbers and resources. I need not tell the survivors of so many hard-fought battles, who have remained steadfast to the last, that I have consented to this result from no distrust of them; but, feeling that valour and devotion could accomplish nothing that could compensate for the loss that would have attended the continuation of the contest, I have determined to avoid the useless sacrifice of those whose past services have endeared them to their countrymen. By the terms of the agreement, officers and men can return to their homes and remain there until exchanged. You will take with you the satisfaction that proceeds from the consciousness of duty faithfully performed; and I earnestly pray that a merciful God will extend to you His blessing and protection. With an increasing admiration of your constancy and devotion to your country, and a grateful remembrance of your kind and generous consideration of myself, I bid you an affectionate farewell.

R. E. Lee, General

* Interesting assignments *

When was Lee given the overall command of the Southern army?

What is the interesting coincidence regarding the surrender taking place in Major McLean's parlor?

What happened to Jefferson Davis, president of the Confederacy, after the surrender?

Battle Summaries — Chapter 3

1861 — CIVIL WAR BATTLE CHART — 1865

BATTLE	DATES	LOCATION	COMMANDING OFFICER Southern	COMMANDING OFFICER Northern	RESULTS	INTERESTING FACTS
Firing Upon Ft. Sumter						
Battle of Bull Run/ Manassas Junction						
Monitor and *Merrimac* Duel						
Shiloh Campaign						
Second Battle of Bull Run						
Antietam/ Sharpsburg Battle						
Vicksburg Campaign						
Battle of Gettysburg						
Surrender at Appomattox						

CREATING A TIMELINE
Chapter 4

With many notable events concerning the Civil War, creating a chronological timeline will help the students achieve a prospective of related occurrences. When any study is systematically organized in this fashion, it makes a more lasting impression.

Any type or size of paper may be used, but I have found that the butcher paper which comes on an 18 inch roll works best for this project. Select a beginning and an ending date, such as 1860 - 1865. Draw a horizontal line across the middle of the paper and divide this line into sections and subsections representing the time periods which you are covering. Because of the multitude of significant events occuring during each year, the subsections should not reflect a time period of more than six months, and three month subsections would be preferable. Above the line cite only events which pertain to the Civil War. Below the line note any other events you discover which were contemporaneous to the war. I highly recommend the use of *Timetables of History* (Grun, Bernard. Simon & Schuster, 1991) in order to help supply the needed information for the timeline. This book can be found in most public libraries.

This timeline can be completely handmade with all entries handwritten, or you can create the information on a computer and paste it onto the timeline. Adding pictures to the timeline is a nice touch. Using symbols that represent such events will help one get an overall picture of what took place. Suggested symbols are as follows: Northern/Southern victories, (blue and silver stars); Naval battle (boat); Inventions and Discoveries (test tube); People (outline of man); Literature (book); and others you deem appropriate. Several pages of dates and events pertaining to the Civil War and sorted both chronologically and alphabetically are included in this chapter. Should your students research their ancestors and find anything relevant to the study, be sure they include this on the timeline.

An alternate to using continuous paper from a roll is to use computer paper that is attached by perforations. A timeline made on this type of paper can be easily folded and kept in a portfolio.

A sample of how to set up your timeline is given on the following page.

Creating A Timeline   - 44 -   **Chapter 4**

    Also included in this chapter are reproducible black-lines for your use when making a timeline. Debora McGregor has put together a book entitled *A Garden Patch of Reproducible Homeschooling Planning & Educational Worksheets* (ordering information included in the bibliography). This book includes many forms (including several timelines) that you may wish to reproduce for your students.

    Following the black-lines, you will find a list of dates and events pertaining to the Civil War.

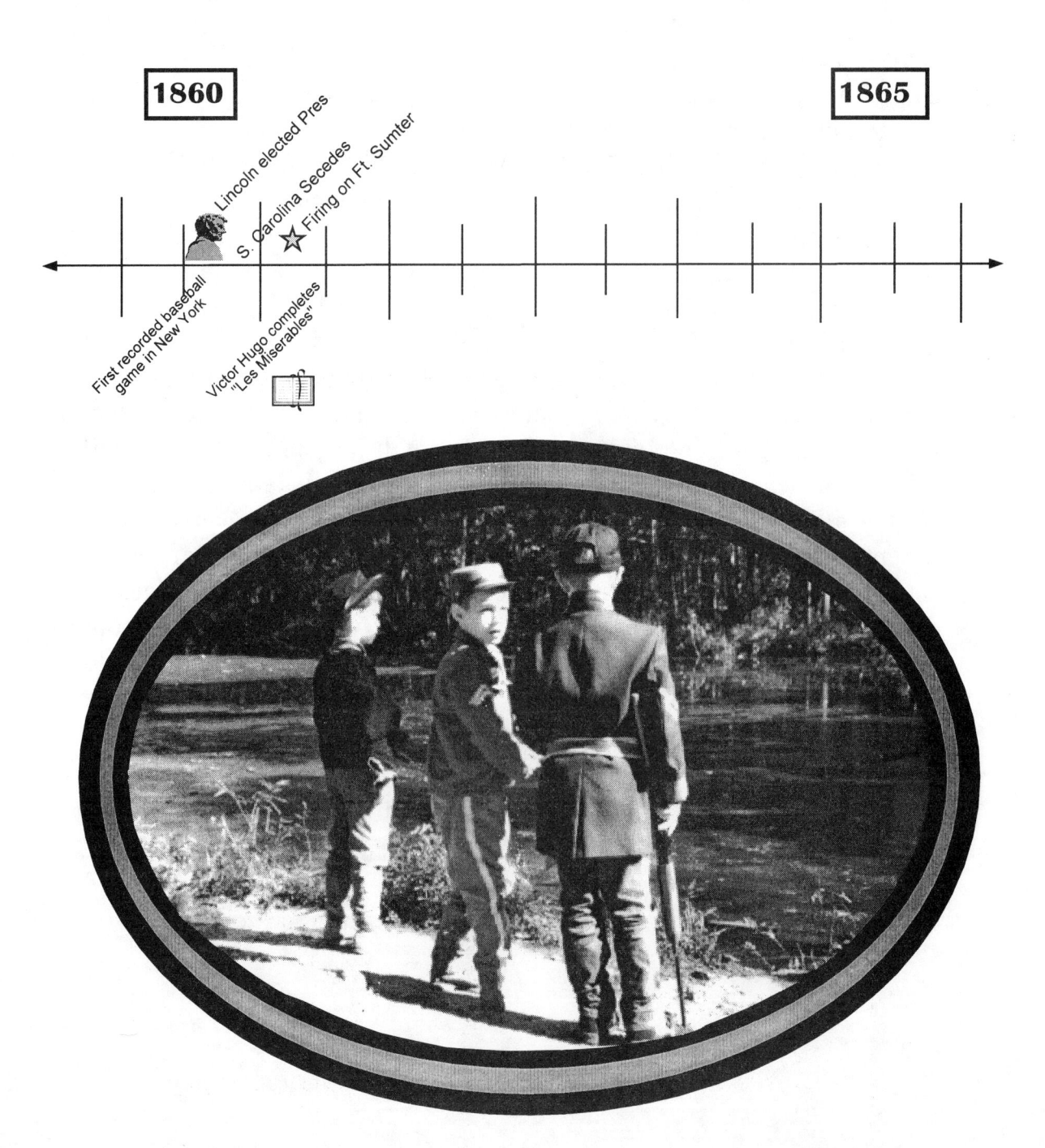

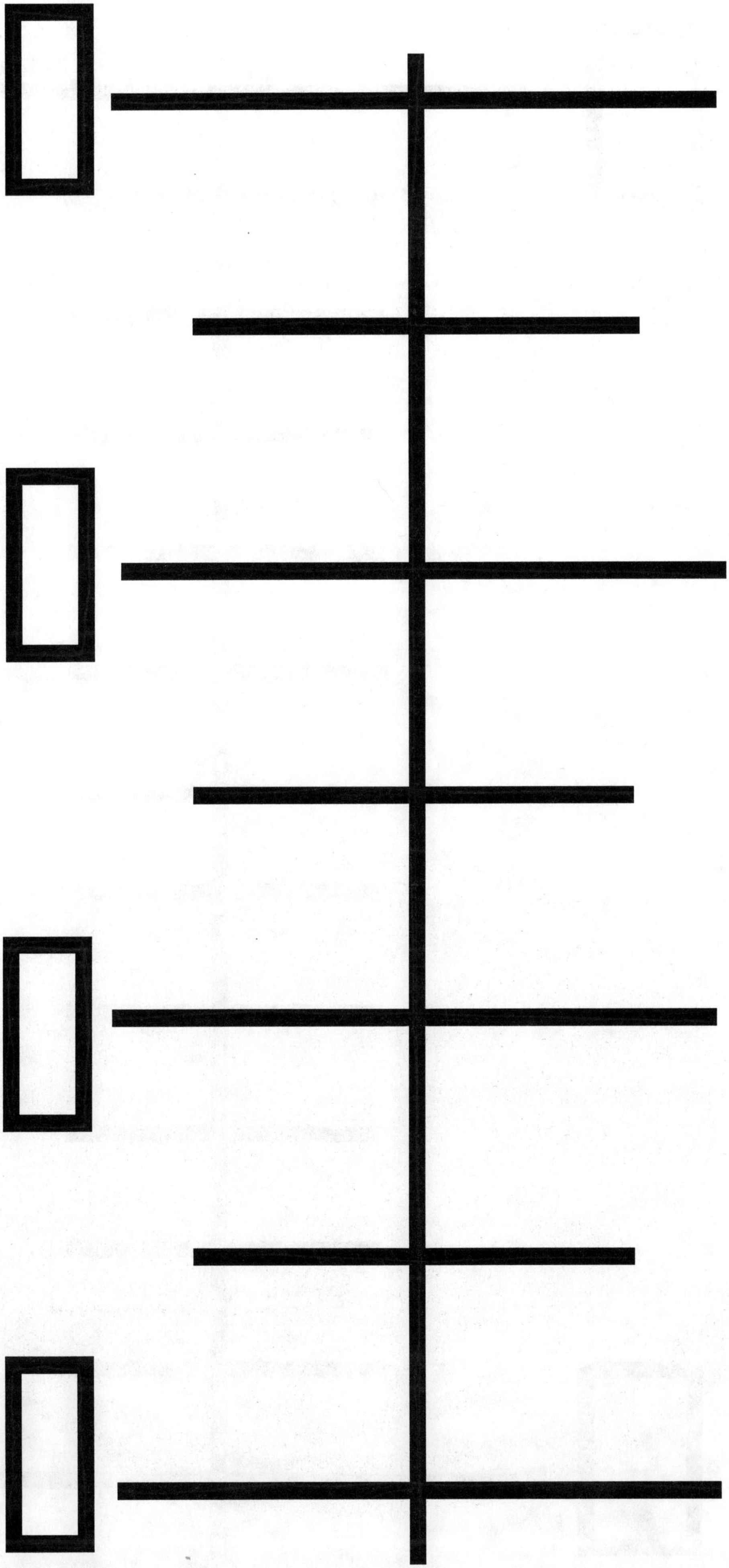

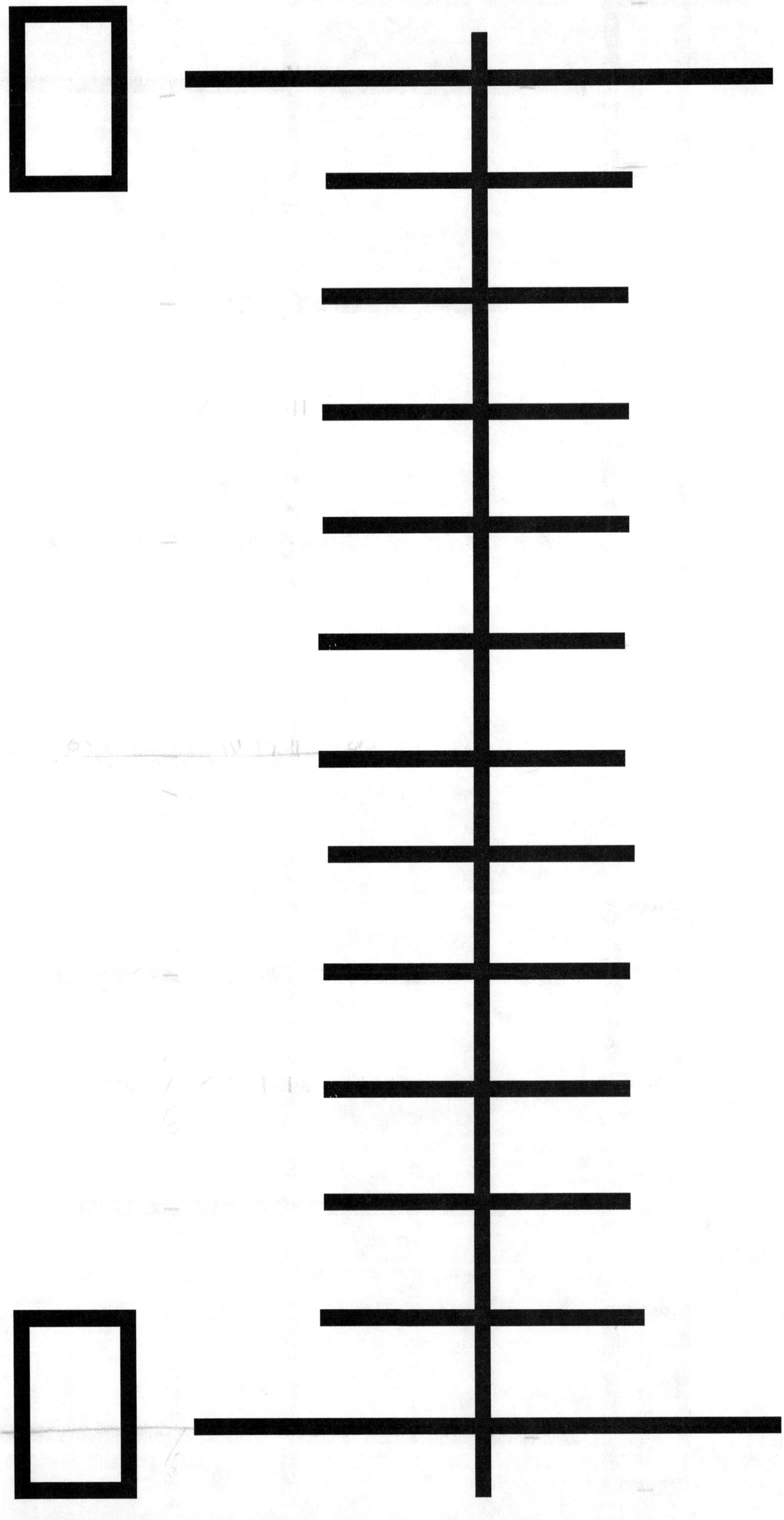

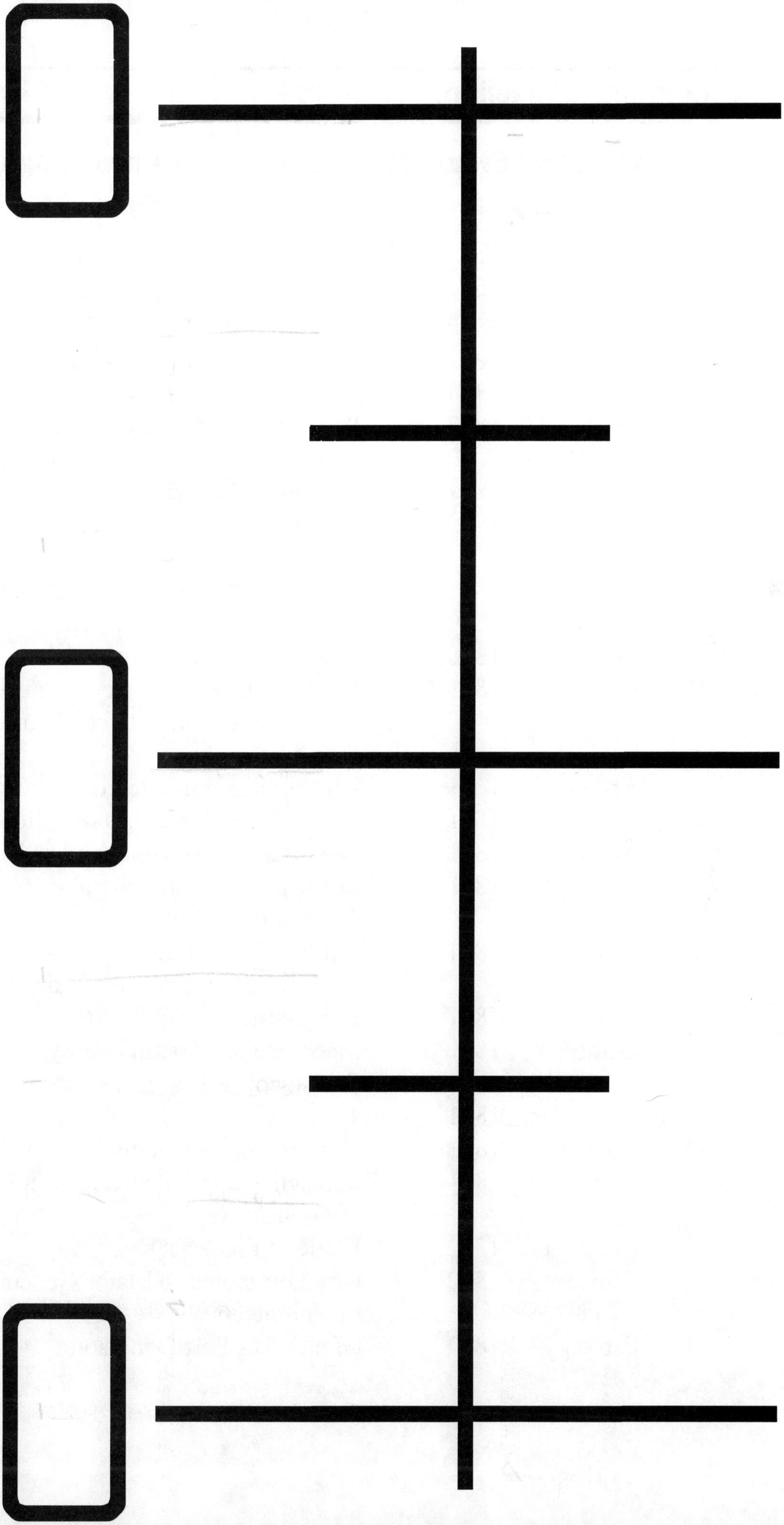

Dates and Events of Interest Sorted Chronologically

		1845	Texas entered as slave state
		1849	Harriet Tubman escapes slavery
		1850	Compromise of 1850
		1852	*Uncle Tom's Cabin* written
	April	1854	Grant resigns from army
	May	1857	Pottawatomie Massacre - John Brown kills 5 pro-slavery men
		1857	Dred Scott Decision
	October	1859	Harpers Ferry stormed and John Brown captured
	April	1859	"Dixie" penned by Daniel Decatur Emmett
	December	1860	South Carolina secedes from the Union
	November	1860	Lincoln elected President
18	February	1861	Jefferson Davis inducted into office as CSA (Confederate States of America) President
13	April	1861	Fort Sumter surrendered
15	April	1861	Lincoln calls for end to rebellion
18	April	1861	Lee offered field command of Union Army
	June	1861	Lee appointed full general in Confederate Army
18	June	1861	Balloon *Enterprise* dispatches first telegraphed message from air
20	July	1861	First Battle of Bull Run/Manassas
	October	1861	Machine gun, first in history to be ordered (by Lincoln)
8	November	1861	Trent Affair
11	November	1861	Scott retired as Commander of U.S. Army
	November	1861	McClellan appointed Commander in Chief of U. S. Army
	December	1862	Battle of Fredericksburg
	February	1862	Grant promoted to Major General of Volunteers
	February	1862	Grant takes Fort Donelson

17	March	1862	McClellan relieved of duty as Commander in Chief of U.S. Army
8	March	1862	*Monitor* and *Merrimac* (*Virginia*) clash
	April	1862	Battle of Shiloh
1	July	1862	Battle of Malvern Hill
	August	1862	Second Battle of Bull Run/Manassas
	September	1862	Union attacks Burnside Bridge
	September	1862	Battle of Antietam
	September	1862	Emancipation Proclamation issued by Lincoln
	September	1862	Lee's troops enter Maryland
	October	1862	Lincoln relieves McClellan of duty until further ordered
	January	1863	Emancipation Proclamation takes effect
	April	1863	Seal of Confederate States of America adopted
	May	1863	Battle of Chancellorsville
2	May	1863	Stonewall Jackson dies
	July	1863	Lee invades Pennsylvania
	July	1863	New York draft riots
1	July	1863	John Reynolds, (general) dies
	September	1863	Battle of Chickamauga
19	November	1863	Gettysburg Address delivered by Lincoln
17	February	1864	First successful submarine attack
	March	1864	Grant appointed Commander in Chief of all the Union Armies
12	May	1864	J.E.B. Stuart dies from wounds received at Battle of Yellow Tavern
3	June	1864	Battle of Cold Harbor
4	July	1864	Siege of Vicksburg
	September	1864	Fall of Atlanta
1	September	1864	Rosie O'Neal Greenhow, famous spy, found dead after trying to swim to shore
	November	1864	Atlanta burned
	November	1864	Lincoln reelected President of U.S.
	December	1864	Sherman's march to sea begins
	February	1865	Lee named General in Chief of all Confederate Army

| Creating A Timeline | - 50 - | Chapter 4 |

4	March	1865	Final Confederate National flag adopted
2 - 3	April	1865	Petersburg, Seige of
9	April	1865	Lee surrenders to Grant at Appomattox
14	April	1865	Lincoln shot at Ford's Theatre
23-24	May	1865	Grand Review of Armies in Washington
24	August	1866	U.S. Army becomes first to adopt a machine gun (Gatling's)
	November	1868	Grant elected President of U.S.

Jonathan, Richard and Allen Gerrell

Events Sorted Alphabetically

	November	1864	Atlanta Burned
18	June	1861	Balloon Enterprise dispatches first telegraphed message from air
	September	1862	Battle of Antietam
20	July	1861	Battle of Bull Run/Manassas, First
	August	1862	Battle of Bull Run/Manassas, Second
	May	1863	Battle of Chancellorsville
	September	1863	Battle of Chickamauga
3	June	1864	Battle of Cold Harbor
	December	1862	Battle of Fredericksburg
1	July	1862	Battle of Malvern Hill
	April	1862	Battle of Shiloh
22	February	1862	Confederate States of America organized
		1850	Compromise of 1850
18	February	1861	Davis, Jefferson inducted into office as CSA President
	April	1859	"Dixie" penned by Daniel Decatur Emmett
		1857	Dred Scott Decision
	January	1863	Emancipation Proclamation goes into effect
	September	1862	Emancipation Proclamation issued by Lincoln
4	March	1865	Flag adopted (final), Confederate National
13	April	1861	Fort Sumter surrendered
19	November	1863	Gettysburg Address delivered by Lincoln
23-24	May	1865	Grand Review of Armies in Washington
	March	1864	Grant appointed Commander in Chief of all the Union Armies
	November	1868	Grant elected President of U.S.
	February	1862	Grant promoted to Major General of Volunteers
	April	1854	Grant resigns from army

	February	1862	Grant takes Fort Donelson
	October	1859	Harpers Ferry stormed; John Brown captured
2	May	1863	Jackson, Stonewall dies
	June	1861	Lee appointed full general in Confederate Army
	July	1863	Lee invades Pennsylvania
	February	1865	Lee named General in Chief of all Confederate Army
18	April	1861	Lee offered field command of Union Army
9	April	1865	Lee surrenders to Grant at Appomattox
	September	1862	Lee's troops enter Maryland
15	April	1861	Lincoln calls for end to rebellion
	November	1860	Lincoln elected President of U.S.
	November	1864	Lincoln reelected President of U.S.
	October	1862	Lincoln relieves McClellan of duty until further ordered
14	April	1865	Lincoln shot at Ford's Theatre
	November	1861	McClellan appointed Commander in Chief of U. S. Army
	March	1862	McClellan relieved of duty as Commander in Chief, U.S. Army
	October	1861	Machine gun, first order in history (ordered by Lincoln)
8	March	1862	*Monitor* and *Merrimac* (*Virginia*) clash
	July	1863	New York draft riots
2 - 3	April	1865	Petersburg, Siege of
	May	1857	Pottawatomie Massacre where John Brown kills 5 pro-slavery men
1	July	1863	Reynolds, John (general) Dies
1	September	1864	Rosie O'Neal Greenhow, famous spy, found dead after trying to swim to shore
11	November	1861	Scott retired as Commander of U.S. Army
	April	1863	Seal of Confederate States

Creating A Timeline — Chapter 4

	April	1863	Seal of Confederate States of Ameria adopted
	December	1864	Sherman's march through Georgia begins
	December	1860	South Carolina secedes from the Union
12	May	1864	Stuart, J.E.B. dies from wounds received at Battle of Yellow Tavern
17	February	1864	Submarine, first successful attack
		1845	Texas entered U.S. as Slave State
8	November	1861	Trent Affair
		1849	Tubman, Harriet escapes slavery
24	August	1866	U.S. Army becomes first to adopt a machine gun (Gatling's)
		1852	*Uncle Tom's Cabin* written
17	September	1862	Union attacks Burnside Bridge
4	July	1864	Vicksburg, siege of

Sarah with sister, Rachel

Let's Debate the Issues
Chapter 5

Conducting a formal debate will give your students invaluable public speaking experience. An official debate simply requires a mediator and two people who hold opposing views. The more people involved in the debate, however, the livelier it becomes. When we had our students debate, we let those who had a preference pick the side which they wanted to defend (North or South). Those without any preference were assigned to a team. For your debate try to keep the teams equal as far as number and ages of students.

To prepare for your students' debate, begin by discussing the Lincoln/Douglas Debate (1858). Discuss with your students some of the occupations which require debating skills such as politicians and lawyers. Finally, be sure that your students understand the definition of a debate. While a debate can take on many different forms, it is the presentation of arguments "for" and "against" a certain position.

Watch a previously televised debate between political candidates and have the students note if any of the statements are completely ignored and left without rebuttal. Also have them note how the subject may change mid-stream in order to suit the person who is responding. Survey the upcoming topics on Nightline (ABC at 11:30 p.m. Eastern Time) and select for viewing a show that will feature guests with opposing views. Tape the broadcast and show it to your students.

You may wish to assign one or more of the students to cover your debate and write an article for the newsletter.

Generally, in a formal debate, one team is called the "affirmative" side and the other, the "negative." The debate opens and closes with the affirmative side. After opening assertions are made (in which the debating sides state their premises), each side is then given an opportunity to rebut the remarks made by their opponents. If several issues will be debated, they should be addressed one at a time. Once a new issue has been introduced, then issues previously debated are no longer open for further discussion or rebuttal.

The role of the mediator (which can be a student or parent/teacher) is to maintain order. The mediator makes sure that each side has an opportunity to respond to a remark at least once before going on to another subject. The mediator determines and explains the rules (who speaks first, time limits, and such). You may want to appoint judges to appraise and declare the "winner" (we did not include judging as part of the debate, feeling it was beyond the scope of our intended purposes). The students should not be allowed to name-call or make non-factual offensive remarks. There is flexibility in how you conduct your debate. Consult a book such as *Warriner's English Grammar and Composition* for more information in this regard.

You may wish to divide the topic of the Civil War into several areas and debate these issues separately. The issue you choose to debate will be your "proposition." A proposition is a topic stated in debatable form. It should contain only one central idea yet be debatable. The proposition should be stated fairly and affirmatively. It should put the burden of proof on the affirmative. Some of your choices for a proposition might be:

1. Did the South have the Constitutional right to secede?

2. Was the North responsible for the influx of slaves into the U.S.?

3. Did the Civil War begin because of slavery?

4. Is slavery wrong?

5. Was President Lincoln an abolitionist?

Begin by having your students first research the subject (as determined by the proposition), learning as much as possible about both sides. Next, after discarding information which is irrelevant to their thesis, they should narrow down the primary issue into the chief points of disagreement between the two sides. Finally, the students should compile supporting evidence for their position as well as evidence which would rebut the opponents' arguments. After researching the subject, your students may discover that their previously held beliefs are not tenable with their newly found evidence.

Often statements are made with no factual foundation whatsoever or are based on "partial" truth. Neither repetition of a lie nor popular

Let's Debate the Issues — Chapter 5

support of one will make it true. Now might be a good time to discuss *Uncle Tom's Cabin*. Where did Harriet Beecher Stowe get her information on the treatment of slaves in the South? Many minds have been influenced by this book, yet historians are now questioning the accuracy and fairness of her portrayal of Southern slave owners.

There is also much controversy about John Brown. Was he a hero or a murderer? Have your students research these controversial issues and write articles for the newsletter reporting their findings. Doing so will give them a feel for how there are many sides to the same issue.

On the day of the debate, set up two tables facing each other. Attach a banner to each table signifying the position of each team. Provide name tags for those participating in the debate (including the mediator). The mediator will need a stopwatch and, if possible, a podium.

To begin the debate the proposition is read to the group. A debate is divided into two parts. During the first part both sides present their arguments for or against the proposition. You may want to have a short break before proceeding with the second part when both sides try to refute the opposing arguments.

Ridicule, sarcasm, and personal attacks have no place in debating. A debate should be won or lost on the basis of reasoned argument and convincing delivery.

Before accepting statements made as "fact," your students should ask their opponents some of the following questions:

1. What do you mean by _____? (Define your terms.

    Be sure you are comparing apples with apples.)

2. How do you know that to be true?

3. On what information do you base that statement?

4. Where did you get that information?

If you are pleased with the debate, you may want to have your students repeat it in front of a larger class or group of people in order to get the feel of a live audience. Video taping the debate and replaying it to the students at a later time is also beneficial. Students can better critically analyze their own performance if viewing it from the perspective of an audience.

After the first debate has been completed, schedule another debate but this time have the students switch loyalties. This will give them the experience of putting themselves into someone else's shoes. Researching both sides of an issue is a vitally important skill.

If you have not yet become convinced, I think that you will soon agree that higher dividends will accrue to those students who "participate" in a debate over those who merely view one.

Allen Gerrell and Kelley

Geography
Chapter 6

The majority of the geography assignments related to this unit study will be concentrated in the eastern United States. As your students research current events of this era, however, they can extend their geographical studies to the rest of the world. Included at the end of this chapter are black line outlines of the United States and of the world. These maps may be copied and used in the assignments listed below.

1. Have your students mark the states and territories that made up the United States <u>prior</u> to the Civil War.

2. Color code the states that sympathized with the North, those that states that seceded with the South, and the states that remained neutral. As your students discover the chronology of each state's secession, have them mark the date of secession on the map.

3. As you study each battle, note its location on the map. Use a silver star to represent a Northern victory and a blue star to represent a Southern victory.

4. Allow your students to select a regiment and follow its course during the war, plotting on a separate map the battles in which the regiment you selected took part.

5. When your students research events contemporary with the war, let them date and identify the location of each event on a world map. For instance, Victor Hugo authored *Les Miserables* in 1862. Affix a small label on France, making note of this. Self-adhering dots, obtainable from most office supply stores, work well. Color coding of these labels (blue dots for inventions and yellow dots for literature) may be utilized for this purpose.

6. Have a separate world map to use for the battles that took place at sea. There were several battles involving ships that occurred outside United States territorial waters.

7. On another map note the locations of the Northern blockades and trace the route of the ships that ran the blockades.

8. Mark the common routes that the "underground" railroad used in order to help slaves escape to the North.

9. Research the locations of the forts, who had original control of the fort, and "if" and "when" the fort changed hands. Place this data on several maps, dividing the war into time periods (six months or a year) in order to show the change of possession that occurred.

10. Identify the locations of the prisons held by both sides during the Civil War. Note on the map the location of the largest prison held by each side.

11. Have each student, or group thereof, draw an enlarged map of any particular state and list the significant events occuring in that state.

12. Research your ancestors' involvement in the war (if applicable) and mark on a map the location at which their participation took place.

13. Find out which battles were the costliest in terms of casualties and mark these on a map, numbering them from one (with the most casulaties) through ten.

14. Some deserters were known to have relocated to other countries. Additionally, many Southerners left the United States after the war, taking up residence elsewhere. As you discover such individuals during your research, note their identity as well as the country to which they found refuge.

15. Put a label on each state involved in the war and record the total number of men from that state who participated in the war.

16. Repeat #15 above, but instead record the number of casualties that each state suffered.

17. On a separate map, mark the location of the capitals of both sides, as well as other pertinent landmarks (such as ammunition factories, hospitals, etc.).

18. Study the courses of famous officers, marking the route that their armies took. Estimate and record the number of miles these men marched.

19. The railroads played an important role in the war. Mark the railroads that <u>existed before</u> the war, those <u>built during</u> the war, and the ones <u>destroyed during</u> the war.

20. Chart on a map the route of Sherman's march from Tennessee to Atlanta and on toward his march to the sea.

United States

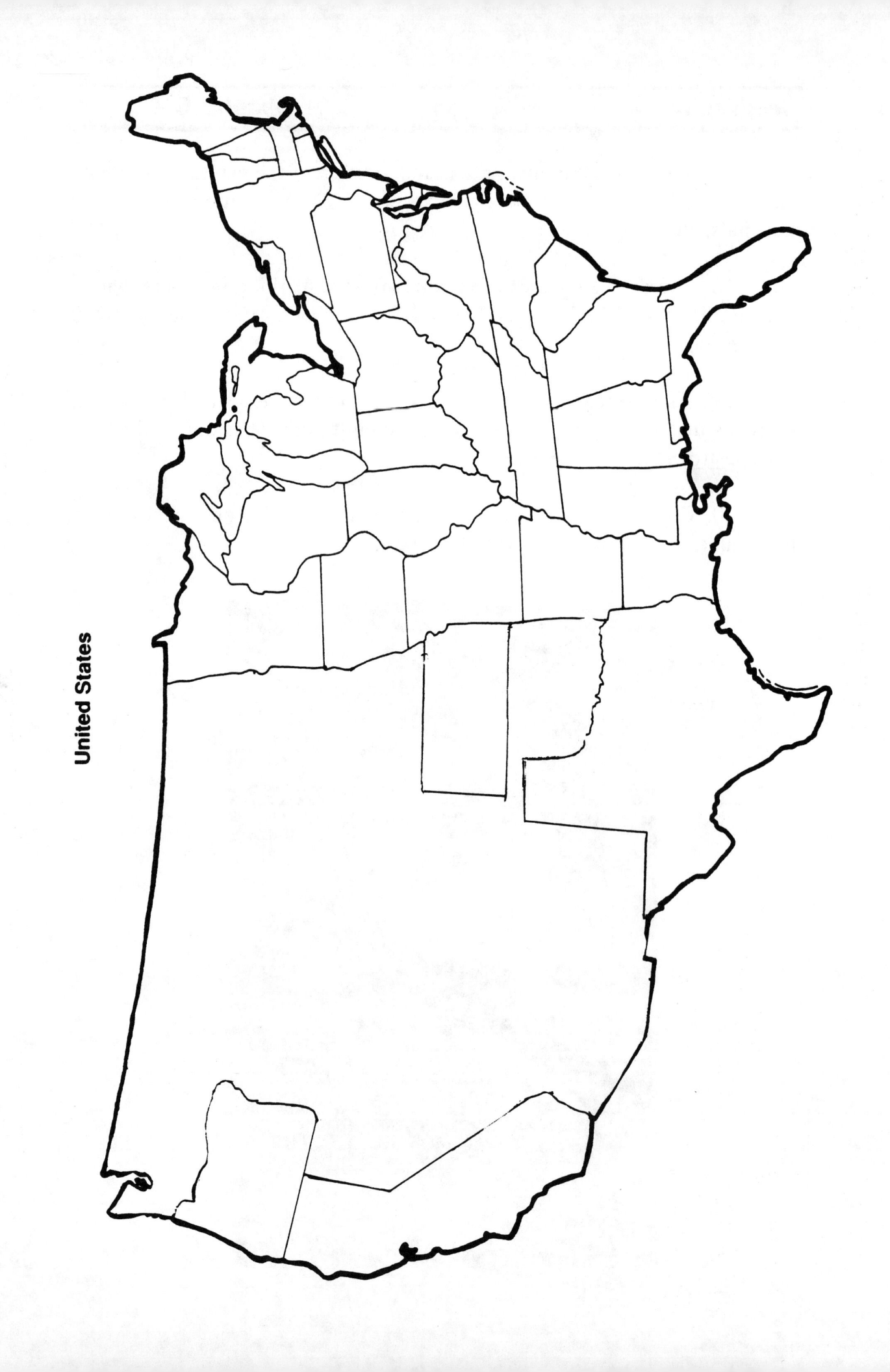

World

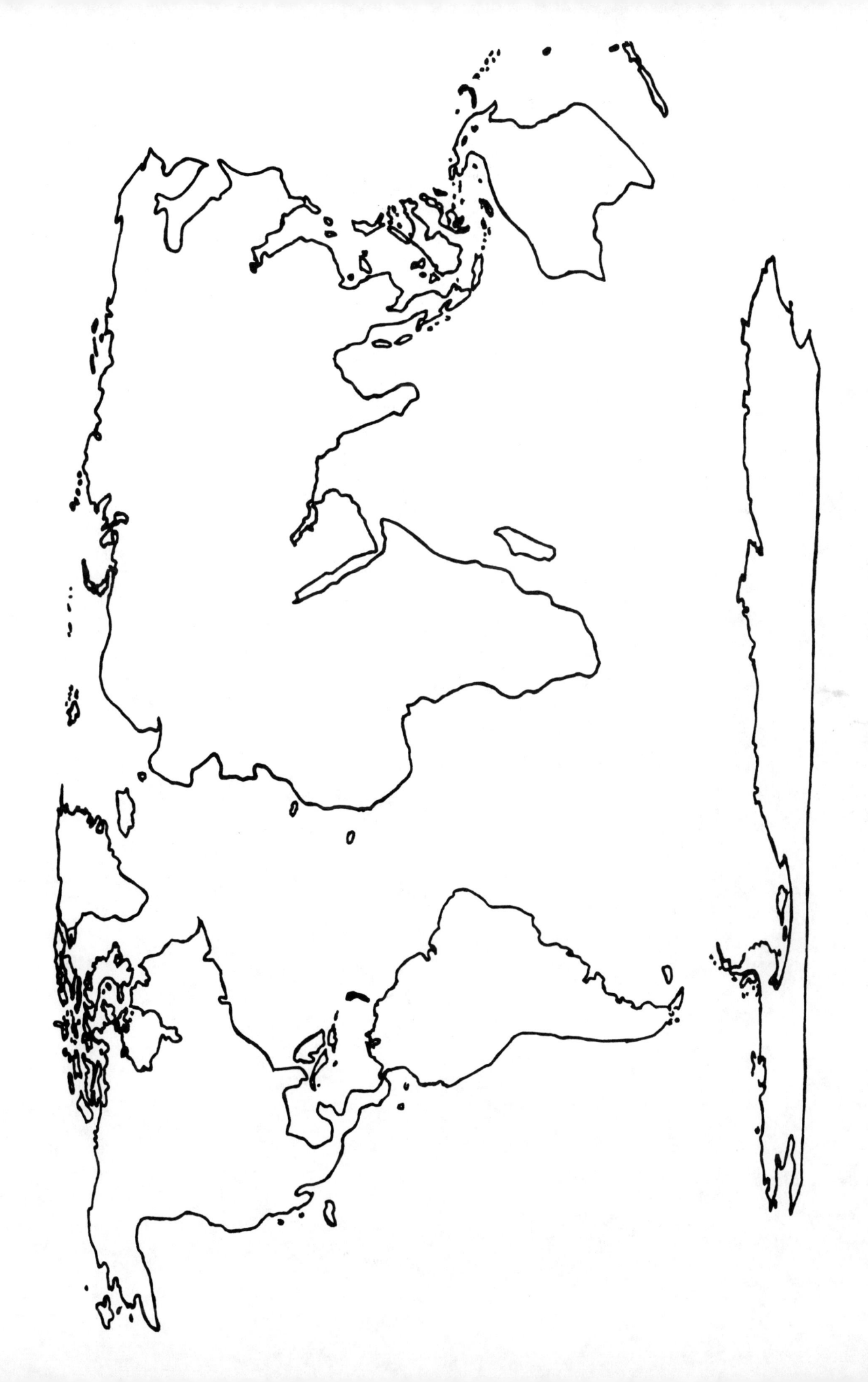

Literature/Language Arts
Chapter 7

Many types of literature written have been inspired by the Civil War. Selections seem endless, and by reading a variety of them, your students will be exposed to many writing styles and techniques while enriching their vocabularies with new words. Have the children keep a list of unfamiliar words in their notebooks along with the definitions (which they should research). As an alternative to a vocabulary list, your students can keep an alphabetized card catalog of words and definitions which will make indexing easy. The repetition of writing new words will increase their recognition and understanding of these words; thus expanding their vocabulary and ability to effectively communicate.

When your group meets together, assign someone (student, parent or teacher) to read excerpts from various types of literature pertinent to the study and/or time period of the Civil War. Select literature that is interesting yet different from the previous week's choice. For example, *Company Aytch* (Sam R. Watkins, New York: Macmillan Publishing, 1962) is a book of memoirs written by a Southern private two years after the war ended. Although it might not be considered a literary masterpiece, it has a unique style that is compatible with the times. Reading a portion of *Uncle Tom's Cabin* is a great way to start a discussion. Mary Boykin Chestnut is famous for the diary that she wrote during the war. It has an abundance of descriptive observations of both Southern life and its leaders. General Robert E. Lee's letters sent home have been published, as have General Sherman's letters, and those of many other officers and privates on both sides of this conflict. These give tremendous insight into this historical period and make for very interesting reading. The Bellerophon, Dover and Scholastic companies have published excellent children's books about the Civil War. These books are inexpensive, ranging in price from $1.95 to $5.95. One of my favorites is entitled *Pink and Say* (Patricia Polacco, New York: Scholastic, 1995). It is a moving and true account of a fifteen-year-old boy who was wounded and left for dead, only to be found and saved days later by a black soldier (also a boy). The story is highly emotional and while the ending is sad, your students will empathize with the boys and their involvement in this war.

Exposing your students to different types of literature will also spur their creativity when they write the newsletter articles that you will be publishing. During your readings, be sure to include several poems and songs, since they carried strong messages too. When sharing excerpts from literature at your weekly gatherings, discuss the methods which the author employed to retain the reader's interest (i.e., how did he keep the story exciting? What words did he use to increase your desire to know more?) As your students witness different techniques modeled, they will begin to incorporate some of the same in their writings. As an optional writing assignment, have your students mimic the prose, poetry or journalistic style of one particular author and share their renditions with the group.

Should you desire to include spelling as a subject during this study, use the list of vocabulary words for your spelling test. Obviously younger (or less advanced) children will require simpler words than the older children. My personal experience reveal that a child's spelling improves in direct proportion to his use of words in both reading and writing assignments. Spelling tests give only temporal recollection of these words. The old cliche, "use it or lose it, " applies in this instance.

When discussing the various types of literature that your group will include, categorizing them will be helpful. Explain to your students the qualities that are distinctive in different types of literature (i.e., fiction, non-fiction, biographies and autobiographies, plays, journals, letters, poems, songs and more). When they separate the literature into categories, have them include the author's name, the publisher and the copyright date. A chart is included at the end of this chapter for this purpose.

There are several historical fiction series that touch upon the Civil War. Eugenia Price has two series, one about the city of Savannah and one about St. Simon's Island, both covering this period of war years. Gilbert Morris' *House of Winslow* series has several books that are also set during this time. Have your students compare an excerpt of fact from any of these series with the same historical information provided in a text book. Ask them which account they enjoyed more, and why. Allow one or more students to write an historical fiction account for an upcoming newsletter. Another student might continue the account in a later newsletter. In the event that your students are not yet experienced writers, be sure that they understand the basic elements of a good story — setting, conflict, rising action, climax and denouement (falling action or resolution). Also, discuss their selection of titles and the fact that a good title foreshadows the story. Imaginative titles require thought, and creative writing should include creative titles in order to be successful.

If your students need to brush up on their grammar, punctuation, and other elements of writing, I highly recommend the book, *Write Source 2000* (Patrick Sebranek, et.al.; Wisconsin: Educational Publishing House 1992). This book is impeccably organized and includes a short section for grammar reference. The great writing tips should prove invaluable to your budding writers.

It is worth repeating at this point that the primary advantage of utilizing the unit study method of teaching is the ability to incorporate a myriad of disciplines into one course. The depth of the "language arts" portion can be determined by your goals and your child's abilities and desires. Our group found that the reading aloud of selected excerpts at our weekly meetings, the researching and writing for our newsletter, and the supplemental home reading (between weekly gatherings) was sufficient. While our group study of the Civil War is formally complete, the desire to broaden our understanding of this period in our nation's history has scarcely been quenched. There are too many biographies (and other types of literature) to be read, and the reenactments occurring at the actual battle sites are too alluring to end our study. In fact, the materials that are currently available on this subject are so voluminous that this could become a project of life-long learning.

You too must determine within your time constraints, desires, goals, and other limitations, how detailed or abbreviated your study of the Civil War will be.

Literature/Language Arts — Chapter 7

TITLE OF BOOK	AUTHOR	PUBLISHER	TYPE OF LITERATURE	DATE WRITTEN

Economics and Statistics
Chapter 8

The title of this chapter might intimidate some, but your study in the areas of economics and statistics during the Civil War should generate more than passive interest. If your group involves only younger children, then your coverage of economics and statistics may be superficial. If, however, your group includes high-school-age students, then your study can have some depth to it. There are endless research possibilities and the data retrieved should be plotted on graphs or tables. There are four commonly used types of graphs: pictographs (which use symbols or pictures of objects with a key); pie graphs (which show how parts are related to the whole by percent); bar graphs (which compare items directly); and line graphs (which are best used to show changes or trends over time). Samples are included at the end of this chapter.

One of the primary causes of the South's secession from the North was for economic reasons. The South was almost wholly dependent upon agriculture, and the Southerner had invested everything that he had in his land and his slaves. Take either of these away without remuneration and he was bankrupt. Tilley, in *The Coming of the Glory* says, "What emancipation would involve for this agricultural section was comparable to what would be the economic consequence of a general and permanent strike of all employees of industrial enterprises of New England."

Further economic information as well as statistics will be included in this chapter, but your students will best learn when they research these topics for themselves. Most public libraries have numerous books on hand from which the children can gather the needed information. The following are assignments from which your students may choose to further their study in economics and statistics:

1. Have your students perform a skit illustrating the rise in prices during the war, particularly in the South. Sutlers swarmed the camps when food reserves were low and in demand. Their prices were high; they charged as much as 15¢ a piece for lemons, 40¢ a pound for cheese, and $1 per pint of whiskey. By the end of the war prices in the South were exorbitant, with hens selling at $50 each, butter at $20 per pound and fish at $50 per pair.

2. Divide into groups and have each group research a particular regiment's statistics: number of volunteers, number drafted, number of privates, number of officers, number of casualties (killed, wounded or missing), and number of deserter. Accumulate the information and plot it on one graph.

3. Research the battles and determine the ten costliest battles in terms of casualties and plot the results on a graph. Divide the casualties between killed, wounded and missing if that information is available.

4. Research the geographic locations of the battles and, after dividing the country into sections, record on a graph how many battles were fought in each section.

5. Document the rise in prices of particular products, both in the North and the South, and compare this information on a graph or table.

6. In July of 1862, there was a ratio of one musician to every forty-one soldiers in the war. Research further statistics regarding musicians and include that data on a graph.

7. Of particular interest is the ages of those involved in the war. The youngest boys were typically members of a band. While they were too young to enlist, they still wanted to take part in the action. The young ages of some of the officers is almost unbelievable. After your students have researched this area, have them plot on a graph the ages and total numbers of those involved in the band, as privates and as officers. A good source for some of this information is in the chapter entitled "How Young They Were!" in the book, *The Civil War: Strange & Fascinating Facts* (Burke Davis, New York: Random House, 1960).

8. Also in the book mentioned above, there is a chapter entitled, "The Rains Brothers," which is about the men responsible for making most of the Confederacy's gunpowder. The amount of money spent on weapons and ammunitions is mind-boggling. It is estimated that each Southerner who was shot required 240 pounds of powder and 900

pounds of lead. Research these figures and plot them on a graph. Compare the amount spent by the North verses the South. Some intriguing questions to discuss are the following: "If all the money spent on ammunitions and weapons during the war had instead been used to purchase the freedom of the slaves, at fair prices to the owners, what would the cost difference be? Would this have been a viable alternative to war?"

9. Where did the finances come from that funded both sides? How did the South continue to raise the needed funds to finance their war effort? How much money did each side spend during the entire time span of the Civil War? What happened to the debts remaining in the South (if there were any) after the surrender? Research this information and make appropriate tables and/or graphs.

10. John S. Tilley includes many statistics in his books regarding the purchase and sale of slaves, as well as to the number of slaves and who owned them. Have the students make a pictograph of the United States, color coding the states that were largely responsible for the importation and sale of slaves, the states where slaves were owned and the states that wanted to abolish slavery. It is of interest to note that the states which were largely responsible for bringing the slaves to this country were the states that would later favor freeing the slaves. These sentiments, however, came <u>after</u> the slave traders had already made exorbitant profits from this lurid enterprise. Your students might also research the lives of notable officers involved in the war, both Northern and Southern, in order to determine which ones were still slave holders during the war. Ironically, General Robert E. Lee let his slaves have their freedom prior to the war, while General Grant still either owned a slave himself or had family that owned slaves during the war. This research may require various graphs and/or tables in order to include all the pertinent information and comparisons.

11. In 1860, the North had almost 4,000,000 of the foreign-born compared with only 233,000 living in the South. There were some regiments that consisted almost entirely of men who could not even

speak English. Have the children research these numbers and plot the information on a graph.

12. The effectiveness of naval blockades is a subject worthy of study. When did the North begin the use of blockades? How many ships did they successfully block from leaving the country? How many ships did they successfully block from entering the country? How many Southern ships got past the blockade? What are the success rates of the above? How many pounds of cotton were exported and how many pounds were seized? This is information that could easily be graphed once the subject is well researched.

13. As an economic maneuver to end the war, the North counterfeited the Southern currency in massive amounts. They then flooded the South with this bogus money, even duplicating the five-cent notes. How would the circulation of counterfeit money effect the South's economy? Did this have any significance on the war's outcome? Was Southern money accepted from merchants after the war? If their money was not accepted, how did the Southerners purchase needed items after the war?

14. After the war, carpetbaggers and scalawags flooded the South. Who were they, and what part did these men play in reconstruction? Were they beneficial or detrimental to the South?

15. Many Southerners would not accept defeat and refused to continue living in the United States after the war. Have your students research the location where these men emigrated after the war. There is still a large number of people living in Brazil who trace their ancestry to discontented Southern emigres.

16. How many officers had prior battle experience? Although some fought in the Mexican War, there were many others who entered the war with no experience whatsoever. Have your students compare the ratio of officers with battle experience to those without. When they graph their information have them divide their graphs according to

Economics and Statistics — Chapter 8

Northern officers versus Southern officers.

17. Many, many men were captured and kept as prisoners during the war. Some escaped while others died in captivity. What happened to these prisoners at the end of the war? How many prisoners did the North capture, and how many did the South capture? What were the names of the largest Northern and Southern prison camps and where were they located?

18. "The Price in Blood," another chapter from *The Civil War: Strange & Fascinating Facts*, includes many statistics concerning participants in battles, casualties, percentage of loss of regiments and more. As an easier assignment (since all the data is given and no further research is required), have your students plot the given information on the types of graphs of their choice. Compare the completed graphs and discuss the effectiveness of the particular type of graph chosen and used by the students.

19. There were more casualties during the war caused by disease and illness than from actual wounds. Assign a student to research and plot this information on a graph.

20. Although I'm not sure of the availability of this information, have the students research the number of desertions during the war. How many men were apprehended, tried and executed for this crime? How many spies were involved in the war? How many women were used for espionage? How many women were known to have enlisted as soldiers, pretending to be men?

Christina White

Economic and Statistical Information

In 1861, the Northern net caught only one out of ten blockade runners, one out of eight in 1862, one out of four in 1863, and one out of two in 1865.

Cotton could be bought for as little as 3¢ per pound in the South and then sold for 40¢ to $1 in England.

Captains on ships running blockades could earn up to $5,000 per trip.

During the first half of 1861, the entire nail supply of the South was controlled by a few Richmond speculators who caused the price to increase from $4 to $10 per keg.

Salt rose from 1¢ to 50¢ per pound and iron rose from $25 per ton to $1,500 per ton during the war.

It is reported that the War Department spent $4,000,000 a year on bands in 1862, and that there were 618 bands in the service. Discuss whether bands significantly contributed to the war effort on each side. How many slaves could have been freed with the expenditures for these bands?

The Union armies were comprised of the following percentages: men under age twenty-one: 30%; men ages twenty-one to twenty-four: 30%; men ages twenty-five to thirty: 30%; and men over age thirty: 10%.

Louisiana's European Brigade had 2,500 Frenchmen, 800 Spaniards, 500 Italians, 400 Germans, Dutch and Scandinavians, and 500 Swiss, Belgians, English and "Slavonians."

The appropriation for Southern ammunition was initially $20,000 for torpedoes. This rose to $350,000 in 1864, and later to $6,000,000.

Economics and Statistics — Chapter 8

Gun powder successfully coming through the North's naval blockades had risen to $3 per pound by late 1861. By November of that year, however, the South was producing 1,500 pounds of gun powder a day in Richmond and 3,000 pounds per day later at a plant built in Augusta, Georgia. The South saved a substantial amount of money by producing its own powder.

The South smuggled 2,700,000 pounds of nitrate through the blockade for use in the manufacturing of gun powder and produced over 2,750,000 pounds of gun powder at the Augusta plant within three years.

Workmen building the ironclad *Mississippi* earned $3 per day. Postal clerks earned between $700 - $800 annually. Slaves could be hired for $30 a month in 1863. The pay of an Northern private was only $11 per month. The pay for a Southern private rose to $18 per month in 1864.

Of the 425 Southern generals, 77 were killed or died from wounds during the war. Eight Northern generals came from one small town in Illinois (Galena) whose population was only 15,000.

Five hundred forty six nuns are known to have served as battlefield nurses during the war. Of these nuns, 289 were from Ireland, 40 from Germany, and 12 from France.

The final draft of the Gettysburg Address was 269 words long. Five words were one-letter words, forty-six had two letters, forty-four had three, fifty-six had four, thirty had five, twenty-five had six, thirteen had seven and the rest were words with eight or more letters.

The 1st Maine Heavy Artillery sustained a record loss of the war when, in a charge at Petersburg, Virginia (6/18/64), it lost 635 of its 900 men within <u>seven minutes</u>.

At the Battle of Gettysburg, more than 3,000 horses were killed. The 9th Massachusetts lost 80 of its 88 animals.

The Irish Brigade returned to New York after the war with only 1,000 of its 7,000 men.

Of the 3,530 Indians who fought for the North, 1,018 were killed. Of the 178,975 Negro Northern troops, 36,000 men died.

North Carolina was the Southern state which suffered the most number of dead, wounded, and missing, reporting 20,602 casualites (over 13,000 more than any other Southern state).

Of the Northern casualities, 24,866 are attributed to deaths in prisons, and 267 were reported as military executions.

Graph Samples

The information contained in the graphs below is fictional and is only supplied as illustrations of the different types of graphs your students may wish to use. Information can be recorded in different ways and your students should decide the type of graph which best reflects their comparable information.

FACTS: 100,000 men enlisted in the war. 65,000 from the North, 35,000 from the South. The North suffered total losses of 25,000 men while the South lost 15,000 men.

Pictograph

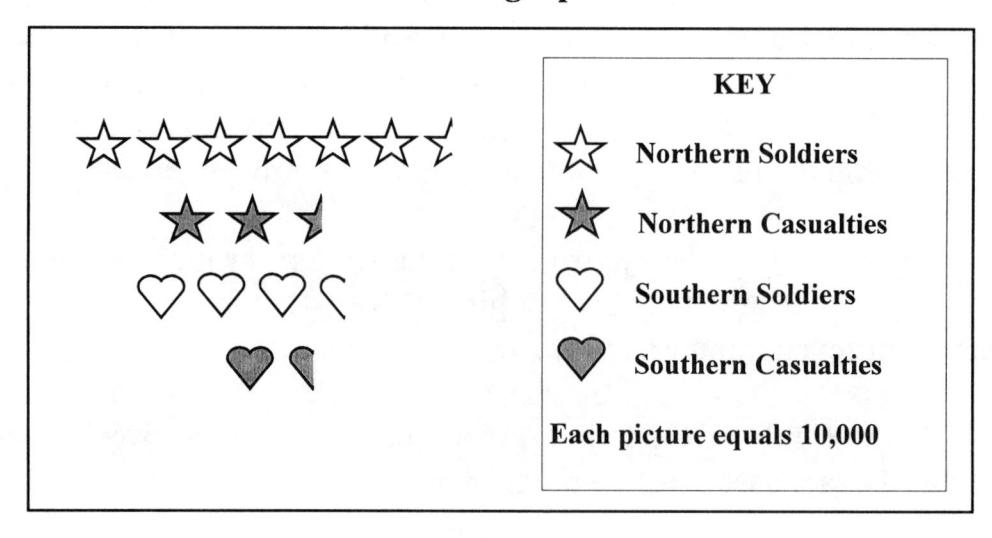

KEY	
☆	Northern Soldiers
★	Northern Casualties
♡	Southern Soldiers
♥	Southern Casualties

Each picture equals 10,000

Economics and Statistics - 77 - **Chapter 8**

Pie Graph

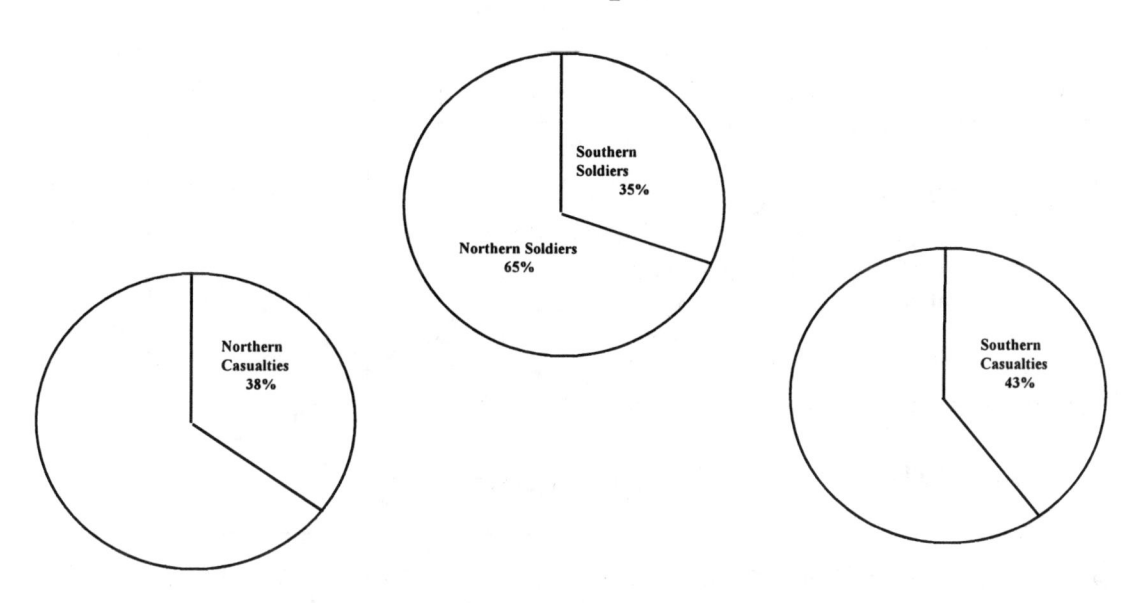

Southern Soldiers 35%

Northern Soldiers 65%

Northern Casualties 38%

Southern Casualties 43%

Bar Graph

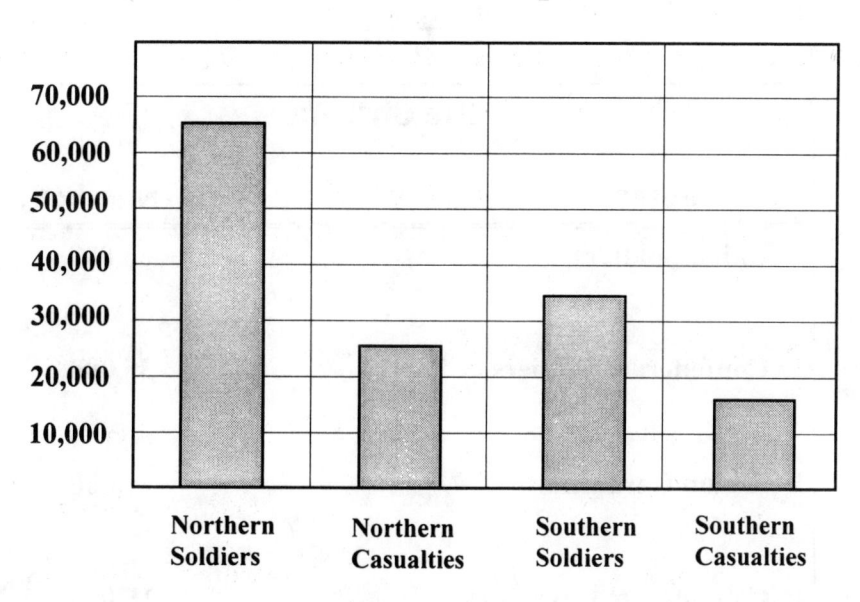

Northern Soldiers	~65,000
Northern Casualties	~25,000
Southern Soldiers	~34,000
Southern Casualties	~16,000

Line Graph

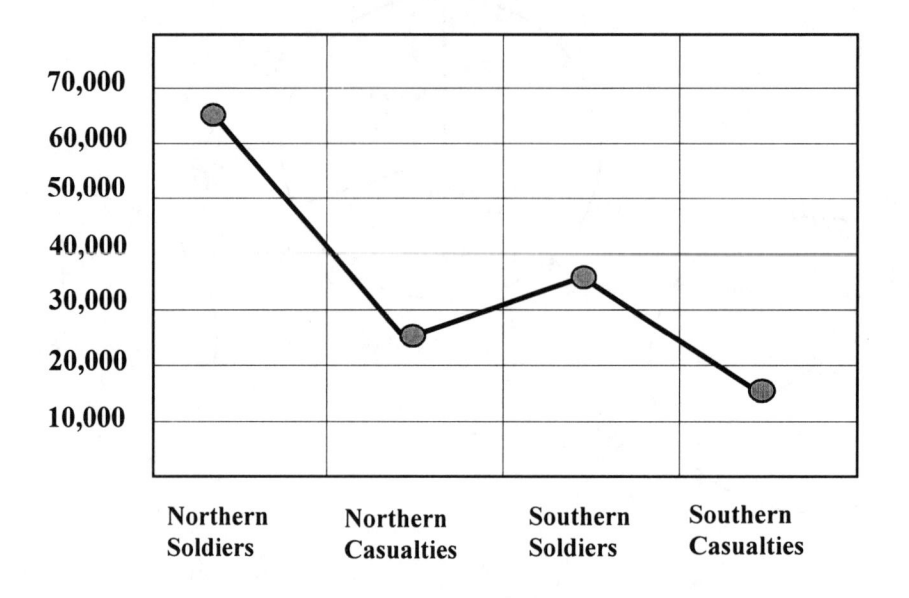

70,000	
60,000	● Northern Soldiers (~65,000)
50,000	
40,000	
30,000	● Southern Soldiers (~35,000)
20,000	● Northern Casualties (~25,000)
10,000	● Southern Casualties (~15,000)

Northern Soldiers — Northern Casualties — Southern Soldiers — Southern Casualties

TABLE

The Civil War	
Subject	**Number**
1. Union Soldiers	65,000
2. Confederate Soldiers	35,000
3. Union Casualties	25,000
4. Confederate Casualites	15,000

Interesting Facts and Famous People
Chapter 9

As I read numerous books during our study of the Civil War, I came across various interesting facts as well as the names of many fascinating people who lived during the war. Discovering this information proved very intriguing. Included in this chapter are a number of items that may spur your students on to further investigation.

The books that I relied on for many of the facts contained herein are as follows: *Timetables of History* (Bernard Grun, New York: Simon and Shuster, q1963), *The Civil War Dictionary*, Dover coloring books, Bellerophon coloring books, *The Civil War - Strange and Fascinating Facts* and *Facts Plus* (Susan C. Anthony, Alaska: Instructional Resources Company, 1995).

The names of individuals referenced at the end of this chapter are listed in alphabetical order. Some of these people were involved directly with the Civil War as officers, scouts, spies, and deserters. Others were alive during the war but weren't necessarily involved with the war. These people include famous authors, poets, artists, Native Americans, inventors, and more. You may want to divide the list of names among the students who are participating in your study. Instruct them to research in order to find out whether the people on their list were or were not involved in the war, where they lived, how old they were during the war and, if they were famous, why? The time allotted to research each name should be governed by the amount of time that you plan to spend on this study and the number of students that are in your group. For example, if you have ten students and your study is going to last ten weeks, then each student should research one or two names each week in order to cover the entire list. The information from this research may be shared in the newsletters which your group publishes.

Interesting Facts

Henry A. Barnum, a Northern general, was believed to have been killed during battle. A body was delivered to his home and a funeral was held. Although he was wounded at Malvern Hill, he didn't die but was taken prisoner and held in Libby until June, 1862.

Elizabeth Blackwell was the <u>first</u> woman to graduate with an M.D. in 1849. She organized, along with her sister Emily, the New York Infirmary for Women and Children.

Andrew Carnegie, steel magnate and public benefactor, served with the Union War Department in the transportation division during the war.

Susan B. Anthony formed the Women's Loyal League in support of Lincoln.

Kit Carson, famed Indian fighter, was a Northern officer.

George Custer had eleven horses shot out from under him and was only wounded once. He was appointed Major General at age twenty-five.

Horace Greeley, one of the first Republican Editors of the <u>New York Tribune,</u> was also one of the signers for Jefferson Davis' bail. This act cost his paper almost <u>half</u> of the subscribers. He was nominated by liberal Republicans for President in 1872, but was defeated by Grant.

Winslow Homer covered the Civil War for <u>Harper's Weekly</u>.

Andrew Johnson, Lincoln's vice-president, only learned to read <u>after</u> his wife taught him.

Because many soldiers did not know their right from their left, their commanding officers would put hay in one boot and straw in the other and order them to march to the order of "Hay foot, straw foot."

The Civil War was the first war to be photographed. Mathew Brady is one of the better-known photographers of the war. It is said that the reason there isn't a photograph of Lincoln giving the Gettysburg Address is because the speech was insufficient in length to allow the shutter to close. Lincoln was in the process of sitting down by the time the picture was taken.

| Interesting Facts and Famous People | - 81 - | Chapter 9 |

Northern infantry men became known as "coffee boilers" because they boiled so much coffee.

Andersonville Prison (a Southern prison located in Georgia) was officially called "Camp Sumter."

The Southern debt to the government at the war's end was two billion dollars.

Jefferson Davis was imprisoned for over two years after the war but was never brought to trial. He was finally released on bail.

The term the soldiers used for their sewing kit was "Soldier's Housewife."

Bounty jumpers were men who enlisted, deserted, and re-enlisted in order to receive money each time they enlisted.

The Southern draft (conscription) was established April 16, 1862, the Northern draft on March 3, 1863.

The longest pontoon bridge constructed used 101 pontoons and was 2002 feet long. It crossed the James River and was used during the Petersburg Campaign in 1864.

Generally speaking, the Northerners named battles after the nearest body of water and the Southerners after the nearest community.

The following is a "Union Soldier's Poem" which was published in the <u>Nashville Daily Union</u> on April 16, 1863:

> The Soldier's fare is very rough,
>> The bread is hard, the beef is tough;
> If they can stand it, it will be,
>> Through love of God, a mystery.

The bloodiest eight minutes of war was during the Battle of Cold Harbor on June 3, 1864. The Northerners suffered a loss of 7,000 and the Southerners a loss of 1,500.

The largest Civil War battle west of the Mississippi was the Battle of Pea Ridge on March 8, 1862. The North won.

Black troops were first used October 29, 1862 at the Battle of Island Mount in Missouri.

The largest calvary battle was the Battle of Brandy Station in Virginia on June 9, 1863. A total of 20,000 troops were involved.

Two American presidents fought at the Battle of Antietam: Lieutenant Colonel Rutherford B. Hayes and Sergeant William McKinley.

The last serious action of the war was the Battle of Palmito Ranch on May 12, 1865, near Brownsville, Texas.

The first battle which Lee and Grant fought against each other was the Wilderness Campaign in May of 1864.

The northernmost land attack by the South took place on October 19, 1864, at St. Albans, Vermont.

The youngest Northern general — Gaulsa Pennypacker — was too young to vote when he became general at age 20.

Colonel Paul Ambrose Oliver of the 5th New York Volunteers invented dynamite after the war.

George Custer was ranked last in his graduating class in 1861.

Paul Revere's grandson was killed at the Battle of Gettysburg.

Interesting Facts and Famous People — Chapter 9

Northern spy Elizabeth Van Lew was called "Crazy Bet" because she pretended to be mentally ill.

Northern spy Pauline Cushman, a professional actress, was captured by the South and sentenced to hang, but was saved by a Southern retreat.

The full name of Southern General S. R. Gist — a native of South Carolina — was "States Rights Gist."

At least two Southern generals were accidentally shot by their own troops — Stonewall Jackson and James Longstreet.

General Nathan Forrest had 29 horses shot from under him.

Southern spy Belle Boyd began gathering information for Jackson in 1862 at age 17.

President Jefferson Davis was blind in his left eye.

"Quaker guns" were used by the Southerners. These were logs that were trimmed and painted to look like cannons.

Stonewall Jackson would not march or fight on Sunday if it could be avoided.

Three high ranking Southern generals were baptized at the end of the war by another Southern general. General Polk baptized Generals Hood, Hardee and Johnston.

Lieutenant Harry Buford was actually a woman — Loreta Velaques. She disguised herself as a man for almost half the war.

The South's most famous cartographer was Jedediah Hotchkiss.

The South's youngest general was William Paul Roberts, age 23.

A Southern dispatch boat, the *America*, which sank off the coast of South Carolina in 1862, was the famous yacht *America,* which won the America's Cup from the British in 1851. It was raised and repaired by the U.S. Navy and in 1870 successfully defended its title.

"Chuck-a-luck" was a dice game played by soldiers during the war.

Most soldiers actually did a lot more sitting than marching or fighting as evidenced by the worn out spots on the rear of their pants.

Stonewall Jackson habitually sucked on lemons, even during battles.

The only gold medal awarded by the U.S. Congress went to General U. S. Grant on December 17, 1863 for his capture of Vicksburg and Chattanooga.

The U.S. War Department offered $100,000 for the capture of Jefferson Davis at the war's end.

The only Native American to become a general in the Southern service was Stand Watie, a Cherokee.

Malinda Blalock disguised herself as Sam Blalock to be in the 26th North Carolina in order to be near her husband, Keith.

General George McClellan's favorite horse was named Daniel Webster.

Northern Officer W.C.P. Breckinridge captured his brother, Southerner J. C. Breckinridge, during the Battle of Atlanta.

On September 6, 1863 two Southern generals, Lucius M. Walker and John S. Marmaduke, dueled. General Walker was killed.

Colonel William Quantrill was a notorious Southern guerilla. In 1864 he headed for Washington to assassinate Lincoln but was fatally wounded by Northern troops in Kentucky.

Two-time deserter John Rowlands (deserting first from the South and then from the Northern Navy) explored Africa under the alias Henry M. Stanley. He uttered the famous query, "Dr. Livingstone I presume?"

The first general to die in the war (and the first Southern officer to die) was Robert S. Garnett of Virginia. He was shot by Federal troops on July 13, 1861, near Carrick's Ford, Virginia.

The last Southern flag to be officially lowered was lowered on November 6, 1865, on the *CSS Shenandoah* at Liverpool, England.

Missouri furnished 39 regiments for the siege of Vicksburg: 17 Southern and 22 Northern.

Rifles were equipped with telescopic sights for the first time during the Civil War.

During the first battle, General Benjamin Butler sent seven Northern regiments to surround and capture Hill's soldiers at Bethel. In the darkness two of these regiments collided, firing on each other. Nineteen were wounded and two were killed.

Abraham Lincoln was encouraged to grow a beard after receiving the following letter from Grace Bedell of Westfield, New York:

> *"I have got four brothers and part of them will vote for you anyway and if you will let your whiskers grow I will try and get the rest of them to vote for you; you would look a great deal better for your face is so thin. . . . All the ladies like whiskers and they would tease their husbands to vote for you and then you would be President."*

On the eve of the battle of Missionary Ridge, Major Noquet, a Southern engineer who had endeared himself to troops by his singing, absconded with $150,000 from the army's money chest. He deserted to the enemy, and told all he knew of Bragg's position.

The best known of all Civil War music began as a call for troops written by Northern General Daniel Butterfield. It is better known as the bugle call "Taps."

Frank Armstrong fought for both sides during the war. He was first a captain fighting with the 2nd U.S. Calvary at Bull Run. He then resigned and went South to become a Southern brigadier general.

The first machine guns used by the North were returned to Washington with a note saying that the guns were "inefficient and unsafe to the operators."

Theodore Roosevelt, at age six, and his younger brother Elliott, watched Lincoln's funeral procession from a second story window on 14th Street.

The first land mines ever used in battle were made by Southerner Gabriel Rains after the earlier design of Samuel Colt.

George Rains sent agents to Europe for more nitrate to help make gunpowder for the Southern cause. He divided the South into districts, each with crews to dig the earth from privies and latrines, and even had them collect the contents of chamber pots — all of which were then dumped into niter beds for processing. This process brought about the singing of some of the war's most entertainingly bawdy songs.

The Rains brothers produced 2,750,000 pounds of gunpowder in three years. Their plant never worked to its full capacity. Once when a rush order came, 22,000 pounds of powder was produced in two days.

Food shortage was a problem for the Southerners. They resorted to killing and eating their mules. Hoping to keep this a secret from the enemy, they realized their practice had been discovered by the Northerners when they appeared on the bank one morning braying loudly.

There is a grave marked in the cemetery of the Lacy family near Chancellorsville that holds Stonewall Jackson's left arm.

George Barhart Zimpleman, a Southerner, probably holds the record for participation in the most battles and skirmishes. He was a private by choice who went through more than four hundred battles and skirmishes, led his regiment in the number of horses shot from under him, and suffered two wounds, one of which crippled him for life.

It has been said that firing was so inaccurate that it took more than a man's weight in lead to kill a single enemy in battle.

The 8th Wisconsin regiment had a mascot unlike any other — an eagle that went by the name of Old Abe. Old Abe hated gunfire and soared high in the sky until the shooting stopped. He followed his master around like a puppy, lived 15 years after the war (although once wounded), and is now on display in the Wisconsin State Museum.

Barnard Family Portrait

Famous People

The following are names of people who lived during the Civil War. Some took part in the war more than others and some had nothing to do with the war at all. This is by no means an exhaustive list. As an interesting research assignment, have your students discover the "who, what, when, and where" of each of these people. Using a chart to fill out necessary information (included at end of chapter) may be helpful.

Louisa May	Alcott
Susan B.	Anthony
Lewis Addison	Armistead
Chester A.	Arthur
Mrs. E. H.	Baker
Clara	Barton
P. G. T.	Beauregard
Grace	Bedell
Mary Ann Ball	Bickerdyke
Antoinette Brown	Blackwell
John Wilkes	Booth
Belle	Boyd
Mathew B.	Brady
Braxton	Bragg
Margaret E.	Breckinridge
James	Bridger
Kady	Brownell
James	Buchanan
John	Burns
Ambrose	Burnside
Andrew	Carnegie
Anna Ella	Carroll
Kit	Carson
Mary Boykin	Chestnut
Grover	Cleveland

Interesting Facts and Famous People — Chapter 9

	Cochise
Buffalo Bill	Cody
Kate	Cumming
Pauline	Cushman
George	Custer
Charles	Darwin
Jefferson	Davis
Emily	Dickinson
Bridget	Divers
Dorothea	Dix
Tom "Dula"	Dooley
Stephen A.	Douglas
Frederick	Douglass
Elizabeth Waring	Duckett
Betty	Duvall
Jubal A.	Early
Wyatt	Earp
Thomas	Edison
Sarah Emma	Edmonds
Ralph Waldo	Emerson
Friedrich	Engels
John	Ericsson
Annie	Etheridge
Edward	Everett
David G.	Farragut
Millard	Fillmore
Olivia	Floyd
Antonia	Ford
Nathan Bedford	Forrest
Stephen	Foster
Barbara Hauer	Fritchie
James	Garfield
Richard	Gatling
	Geronimo

Ulysses S.	Grant
Horace	Greeley
Rose O'Neal	Greenhow
Wade	Hampton
Benjamin	Harrison
Nancy	Hart
Nathaniel	Hawthorne
Rutherford B.	Hayes
Charles	Heidsick
Wild Bill	Hickock
Jennie	Hodgers
Jane	Hoge
Oliver Wendell	Holmes, Jr.
Winslow	Homer
John Bell	Hood
Joseph	Hooker
Julia Ward	Howe
Elizabeth C.	Howland
Victor	Hugo
Horace Lawson	Hunley
Robert G.	Ingersoll
Stonewall	Jackson
Jesse	James
Andrew	Johnson
Rose Roundtree	Kennedy
Black	Kettle
Mrs. William	Kirby
Sidney	Lanier
Robert E.	Lee
Sir Joseph	Lister
Henry Wadsworth	Longfellow
James	Longstreet
T.S.C.	Lowe
Harry	MacCarthy
Lily	Mackall

Interesting Facts and Famous People — Chapter 9

Édouard	Manet
Karl	Marx
George B.	McClellan
Cyrus Hall	McCormick
William	McLean
George	Meade
Mrs. A. M.	Meekins
J. D.	Mills
Virginia	Moon
Charlotte	Moon
John S.	Mosby
John	Muir
Carry	Nation
Alfred	Nobel
Mary	Overall
Dr. William T.	Passmore
Ann & Kate	Patterson
Laura	Pender
Galusha	Pennypacker
George E.	Pickett
Franklin	Pierce
Emmeline	Piggott
James	Plimpton
Ellie	Poole
Gabriel J.	Rains
George	Rains
Laura	Ratcliffe
Belle	Reynolds
J. D.	Rockefeller
Theodore	Roosevelt
William S.	Rosecrans
John	Rowlands
Mary Jane	Safford
Emma	Samson
Winfield	Scott
Raphael	Semmes

William	Seward
Carrie	Sheads
Philip H.	Sheridan
William Tecumseh	Sherman
	Sitting Bull
Elizabeth Cady	Stanton
Billings	Steele
Harriet Beecher	Stowe
J.E.B.	Stuart
Sam	Sweeney
Jacob	Tannenbaum
Susie King	Taylor
George H.	Thomas
Sally Louisa	Tompkins
Sojourner	Truth
Harriet	Tubman
Mark	Twain
Mollie	Tynes
Elizabeth	Van Lew
Loreta Janeta	Velázquez
Jennie	Wade
Mary Edwards	Walker
George	Westinghouse
James McNeill	Whistler
Walt	Whitman
Lucy	Williams
John	Wise
Annie Turner	Wittenmyer
Rebecca	Wright

Interesting Facts and Famous People — Chapter 9

NAME	DATE OF BIRTH	DATE OF DEATH	INTERESTING FACTS

CRAFTS, COOKING, MUSIC AND MOVIES
Chapter 10

Our students' first project was to decorate the folder in which they were going to keep their materials. We used the inexpensive colored folders with pockets and rivets. We bought several of the Bellerophon and Dover coloring books so that the students could color, cut out, and paste pictures on their folder. Captions and dates for these were made on the computer and provided to the students. After the captions, dates and pictures were in place, we then covered the folders with clear contact paper. The notebooks enabled the students to keep track of the published newsletters, reports, completed puzzles, and other materials.

There are many crafts and cooking projects that your student(s) can do. Their creativity is only limited by your time constraints and available funds. Below are a few suggestions that your group might want to consider including in their unit study.

1. Duplicate the flags used during the Civil War. Since flags of this era were numerous, you should ask students to first research this subject and then share with the group the information they have gathered before beginning this project to determine which flags are to be made. Flags can be simply made using only paper and crayons or paper and star stickers. Using felt of the appropriate colors would be another way to duplicate the flags. Painting cloth with fabric paints is yet another option. If you have children who can tackle a complicated sewing project, allow them to utilize this talent by sewing one of the flags used during the war.

2. Make wearable hats similar to those worn by the soldiers. These could be made from construction paper, gluing on insignias (also cut out of paper). Adding insignias to a hat the child already owns is another possibility. Insignias can be purchased from either an *Army and Navy* store or from the sutlers (vendors) at a Civil War reenactment. I found several at a yard sale. As an alternative to buying insignias, they can be made out of felt, masking tape, aluminum foil or other suitable materials. You are only limited by your imagination and available resources.

3. Assemble a full Civil War uniform. When our group planned to meet a reenactor at a battle site, we told the students that they could dress in clothes of this period if they wanted. Most did, and the results were impressive! Masking tape was used to create the stripes down the sides of the soldier's pants and to make the stripes on the sleeves designating rank. Lace-up boots, borrowed from friends and parents (or purchased at second hand stores or yard sales), were worn. The girls wore skirts and blouses as well as mom's old prom dresses with shawls worn around their shoulders. The boys tied sashes around their waists; some wore dad's coat. Although I purchased Civil War caps for my boys, most of the children decorated hats they owned. To top it all off, the boys brought along their play knives, guns and silver plated baby cups (every soldier in the Civil War had a tin cup). If you truly want to add the final touch of realism, allow the kids to bring along their pup tents in order to set up camp.

4. Make candles. Although Civil War soldiers probably did not make their own candles, I'm sure some of the women back home did. Your students would most likely enjoy making authentic "drip" candles. Extreme caution should be observed since the wax will be HOT, but I have personally done this with children as young as five years old, and no one has yet been burned.

To make the candles, melt paraffin wax in a large metal coffee can. If you want your candles to be a particular color, melt a crayon in with the wax. (If you want colored candles, but prefer to use a method authentic to the 1800's, you will have to research this subject and see if that method can be feasibly duplicated.) Purchase enough wick to give each student a piece approximately 10 inches long. You will need a container of cold water equal in size to the can holding the wax. Holding the top of the wick, first dip the string into the hot wax. Lift it straight up out of the can, being careful to allow excess wax to drip back into the can. Then dip the string into the can of cold water, allowing the string to remain in a straight line without bending. Dip it into the wax again, and then into the water. Repeat this process until your tapered candle is the desired thickness. Two children can do this at one time if they are careful to take turns, one using the water while the other uses the wax, and vice versa.

| Crafts, Cooking, Music & Movies | - 97 - | Chapter 10 |

5. Arrange for the children to examine and pick real cotton plants if you live close to, or can conveniently travel to an area where cotton is indigenous. If possible, visit a working pre-nineteenth century village where cotton is processed into thread and then into cloth. If allowed access to the equipment, have the children turn their cotton into thread and/or cloth.

6. Help supervise your students buid a fire outdoors and let them cook a meal on the open fire just as the soldiers did. Boil coffee in cans to drink. Boil feed corn, potatoes, and wild onions to eat. Should your soldiers be fortunate enough to have meat and vegetables, they can even make a stew.

7. Make hard tack or cornbread and molasses cookies to go along with your outdoor meal.

8. Many times the soldiers did not have coffee (particularly the Southerners) so they often made a hot beverage from peanuts, peas, corn, potatoes and/or chicory. Try duplicating and (if brave enough) drinking a concoction made from these ingredients! After doing this your students will understand why it was a happy day for Southern soldiers when they captured rations from their enemies and found "real" coffee!

9. In a pre-approved area, have your children dig a trench using only tin cups. This was often the only tool that a soldier had for digging, and he spent many hours, day after day, digging trenches in preparation for battle.

10. Make haversacks, knapsacks, sewing kits, and ditty bags for the children to use. Choose from felt, burlap, leather or any other materials that you may have on hand to complete these projects. The Bellerophon coloring books entitled *Johnny Reb* and *Billy Yank* include pictures of these items.

11. If you have access to a creek or a stream that is sufficiently

deep, have the children build pontoon bridges using limbs and branches. Adult supervision is needed if the students will be using saws, hatchets, knives or axes.

12. Soldiers had to go for days and sometimes weeks, without the luxury of changing into clean clothes. Have your children wear the same clothes without changing for days. Then let your students hand wash their dirty clothes in a stream (or tub) without the use of soap. Hang the clothes on tree branches or makeshift clothes lines to dry. They will probably gain a real appreciation for our modern conveniences after this. (By the way, make sure that your male students understand this is only a temporary, one-time event. Otherwise, they may want to repeat it every week!)

13. Make full size "wanted posters" as one may have seen during the Civil War. These posters might include escaped slaves, deserters or spies.

14. Have your group assemble a catalog of items that were available for sale during the Civil War period. Include prices as well as the name and addresses of the businesses offering these items. *The Civil War Times* often has articles that include authentic advertisements from the Civil War period.

Movies and Music

Music was very important to the soldier's moral during the war. There is an abundance of music popular today that was either written or popularized during the Civil War period. Some favorites which you may recognize are: *The Battle Hymn of the Republic*, *Yankee Doodle* (which was written prior to the war), and *Goober Peas*. Our local public library has music from this era on compact disc. One of our parents checked this out and played it before our group. There are also several bands that perform authentic Civil War-era songs. Three of these bands sent samples of their music to me. Some of them perform live in Civil War costume and sell reproductions of their music. Feel comfortable contacting them for further information at the following addresses:

Rose of El-A-Noy Minstrels
R. R. 10, Box 289,
Carbondale, IL 62901
Phone (618) 529-3038

97th Regimental String Band
437 Boca Ciega Drive
Madeira Beach, FL 33708
(813) 391-4565

Images
P. O. Box 23221
Toledo, Ohio 43623

One of the best film sources for Civil War information is the public broadcasting documentary produced by Ken Burns. Larger public libraries should have a copy of this series available for you to borrow. This is a lengthy series, but if you watch each of the battles separately while you study them, it won't seem overwhelming. Many movies have been produced concerning the Civil War including *Gettysburg, Gone With the Wind* and *Glory*. My children prefer movies where the battles are reenacted over narrated documentaries. Please be cautious and use discretion since some of these movies are very graphic and include strong language. I suggest that you preview all movies before showing them to your students, editing out portions that you deem inappropriate (or noting when to fast forward through these portions).

We discovered a children's movie at our local library about the underground railroad entitled *Follow the Drinking Gourd*. Being narrated by a black man heightens its sense of realism. This movie was interesting and held the children's attention. One video that wasn't

Crafts, Cooking, Music & Movies — 100 — **Chapter 10**

popular with my family concerned the surrender at Appomattox. It is narrated by an actor being portrayed as Ulysses S. Grant. This too came from the library. The children lost interest almost immediately and I found it difficult to watch the movie to its end. Turner Pictures produced a two-part mini-series about a prison in Georgia entitled *Andersonville* which was recently (Spring, 1996) shown on Turner Network Television (TNT). It is scheduled to run intermittently this year. You may come across a movie not mentioned in this chapter that holds your students' interests and complements this study. If this is the case, please notify me of such and I'll make a note to add it when we reprint this book.

Wesolowski Family Portrait

Puzzles, Games, Codes and More!
Chapter 11

This chapter is included because children love to solve puzzles, play games, break codes, and waste time. The information contained in each one will reinforce the material that they are learning in this study of the Civil War. You may want to distribute these individually as assignments or have them completed in groups. Because this unit study is for children of all ages, different levels of difficulty are included.

DECODE THIS MESSAGE

A	B	C	D	E	F	G	H	I
✌	👌	👍	👎	☞	☜	☝	🖐	✋

J	K	L	M	N	O	P	Q	R
☺	😐	☹	💣	☠	⚑	⚐	✈	☼

S	T	U	V	W	X	Y	Z
💧	❄	✝	†	☥	✠	✡	☪

The first message decodes using the cipher above.

_ _ _ _ _ _ _ _   _ _   _ _ _ _   _ _ _ _ _   _ _   _ _ _ _ _ _.

_ _   _ _ _ _ _ _ _   _ _   _ _ _ _ _   _ _ _ _ _.

_ _ _ _ _   _ _ _ _   _ _ _   _ _ _   _ _ _ _   _ _ _ _ _ _ _ _ _.

Puzzles, Games, Codes and More!

- 102 -

Chapter 11

DECODE THIS MESSAGE

A	B	C	D	E	F	G	H	I	J	K	L	M
♩	𝄡	¢	D.C.	♪	mf		♩	'	♩	♪	⌐	𝄩

N	O	P	Q	R	S	T	U	V	W	X	Y	Z
♫	◊	mp	♩	♪	sf	~	⌒	8ᵃᵇ	⊢⊣	♪	♪	fz

Puzzles, Games, Codes and More!

- 103 -

Chapter 11

DECODE THIS MESSAGE

A	B	C	D	E	F	G	H	I	J	K	L	M
Z	Y	X	W	V	U	T	S	R	Q	P	O	N
N	O	P	Q	R	S	T	U	V	W	X	Y	Z
M	L	K	J	I	H	G	F	E	D	C	B	A

SZIIRVG   RH   SRWRMT   RM   MVD   BLIP.

_____   __   _____   __   ___   ____.

HSV   RH   UIVVRMT   GSV   HOZEVH.

___   __   _____   ___   _____.

GSVIV   RH   Z   SFTV   IVDZIW   ULI   SVI   XZKGFIV.

_____   __   _   ____   _____   ___   ___   _____.

Puzzles, Games, Codes and More!   Chapter 11

Find The Hidden Words

U	N	I	O	N	A	D	F	G	E	N	E	R	A	L	X
A	O	T	S	D	V	G	E	D	I	V	I	S	I	O	N
T	R	O	O	F	S	E	D	A	V	I	S	S	Y	I	V
L	T	M	U	R	G	N	E	R	R	C	L	I	T	S	C
P	H	S	N	O	G	G	R	A	N	T	A	U	R	S	I
C	E	C	A	B	I	N	A	I	T	P	V	F	A	U	V
P	W	O	L	E	I	L	L	L	H	L	E	T	B	E	I
G	U	N	I	R	L	L	I	R	U	I	S	S	A	U	L
E	C	F	N	T	S	I	S	O	N	N	I	U	R	S	W
T	S	E	C	E	D	E	T	A	S	C	E	M	T	U	A
R	R	D	R	L	W	T	S	D	C	O	T	T	O	N	R
O	V	E	E	E	A	P	A	O	L	R	E	N	C	V	
O	L	R	B	E	T	U	B	M	A	N	N	R	N	L	F
P	T	A	T	E	C	B	A	N	D	C	D	T	R	E	R
S	E	T	B	M	L	L	T	Y	V	I	C	T	O	R	Y
L	N	E	P	A	B	E	B	A	T	T	L	E	Y	S	L

Find as many of the words listed below in the puzzle above. They can be horizontal, vertical or diagonal.

UNCLE	TOMS	CABIN	GRANT	CIVIL
SLAVES	SUMTER	CONFEDERATE	UNION	WAR
GENERAL	DAVIS	VICTORY	ABE	TROOPS
FEDERALISTS	NORTH	BARTON	SECEDE	GUN
RAILROAD	TUBMAN	REBEL	ISSUE	DIVISION
LINCOLN	COTTON	ROBERT E. LEE	BAND	BATTLE

Puzzles, Games, Codes and More!

Find The Hidden Words

S	H	I	L	O	H	H	I	L	R	G	M	T
N	S	H	A	R	P	S	B	U	R	G	M	O
T	A	V	E	F	F	T	S	U	M	T	E	R
A	N	T	I	E	T	A	M	C	K	S	R	X
G	T	Y	S	C	B	R	G	E	L	P	R	M
M	A	N	M	E	K	B	U	L	P	P	I	O
Y	E	G	M	N	I	S	T	R	P	G	M	N
P	G	E	T	T	Y	S	B	U	R	G	A	I
J	U	N	B	U	L	L	R	U	N	O	C	T
M	A	N	A	S	S	A	S	E	R	X	K	O
P	M	N	T	I	R	O	S	J	K	G	P	R
X	B	A	P	P	O	M	A	T	T	O	X	T
M	T	L	O	F	J	U	N	C	T	I	O	N

Find as many of the battles listed below in the puzzle above. They can be horizontal, vertical or diagonal.

FT. SUMTER	BULL RUN	MANASSAS	JUNCTION
MONITOR	MERRIMACK	SHILOH	ANTIETAM
SHARPSBURG	VICKSBURG	GETTYSBURG	APPOMATTOX

Puzzles, Games, Codes and More!

Chapter 11

CIVIL WAR CROSSWORD PUZZLE

ACROSS

1. Southern president
2. a stronghold
3. challenged the *Merrimac*
4. Northern general
5. attempt
6. chopping tool
7. Southern general

DOWN

6. Northern president
9. place of surrender
10. not strawfoot
11. first shot fired
12. first fatality of war
13. bloodiest one day battle
15. not a Yank
16. holler

Draw a Line from the Generals to the Side They Represented

Lee

Meade

Hooker

Grant

Jackson, Tom (Stonewall)

Pickett

Sherman

J. E. Johnston

McClellan

Longstreet

Burnside

Stuart, J.E.B.

Buell

Beauregard

McDowell

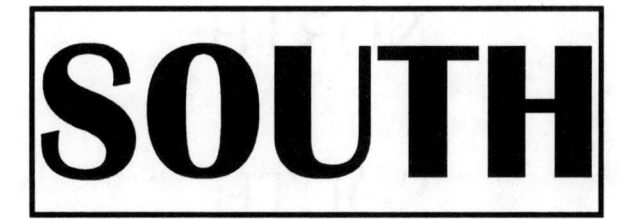

NORTH

SOUTH

Puzzles, Games, Codes and More!

FIND THE HIDDEN WORDS

EASY

G	N	T	C	A	N	N	O	N	S
A	M	G	S	Y	N	H	U	R	T
F	O	R	T	P	L	R	T	S	U
M	M	A	S	T	N	O	R	T	H
O	R	N	H	F	G	S	L	H	H
L	E	T	N	U	O	G	L	F	S
A	G	T	S	O	U	T	H	G	A
R	M	Y	E	E	T	G	R	L	Y
M	N	O	U	T	S	F	L	A	G
Y	R	L	E	E	F	G	G	U	T

NORTH   ARMY

SOUTH   CANNON

FORT   LEE

FLAG   GRANT

Puzzles, Games, Codes and More! — Chapter 11

Find the answer to each problem below then unscramble the letters that are on the bold lines to find the answer at the bottom of the page.

1. The third state to secede from the Union. __ __ **__** __ __ __ __

2. Billy Yank's nemesis __ __ __ __ __ __   __ __ **__**

3. The noise made famous by the South. **__** __ __ __ __   __ __ __ __ __

4. The second speaker at Gettysburg ceremony. **__** __ __ __ __ __ __

5. First Northern ironclad __ __ **__** __ __ __ __

6. South's favorite general __ **__** __

7. Location where the first firing of the war took place. __ __ __ __   __ __ __ __ **__** __

8. Harriet Tubman's underground __ __ **__** __ __ __ __

9. Second location of Southern capital __ **__** __ __ __ __ __ __

Official name of the Civil War.

War of __ __ __ __ __ __ __ __ __

Puzzles, Games, Codes and More!

FIND THE HIDDEN WORDS

B	A	Y	O	N	E	T	A	T	C	V	F	R	L
O	W	A	R	N	E	Y	P	I	A	T	S	L	R
W	S	R	A	M	M	E	R	W	R	I	F	L	E
I	H	R	A	M	R	E	V	P	B	S	F	T	V
E	S	H	F	U	M	R	S	I	I	H	H	V	O
K	L	O	A	T	U	V	T	S	N	L	O	E	L
N	M	W	M	U	S	K	E	T	E	S	L	R	V
I	R	I	I	C	K	T	L	O	I	T	S	S	E
F	A	T	N	A	R	C	U	L	B	E	T	T	R
E	M	Z	I	N	A	A	A	W	A	B	E	L	S
F	R	E	E	N	M	G	F	N	R	A	R	E	O
E	O	R	U	H	S	U	H	W	N	R	S	U	U
T	D	K	S	T	T	N	T	A	C	O	T	O	T
M	D	S	H	O	S	H	O	T	G	U	N	N	H

Weapons and Artillery

MUSKET	BOWIE KNIFE	HOWITZER
RIFLE	PISTOL	RAMMER
BAYONET	CARBINE	RAMROD
MINIE	SHOTGUN	HOLSTER
CANNON	REVOLVER	

FIND THE HIDDEN WORDS

C	A	B	O	N	E	T	A	T	C	S	F	K	L	A
A	W	H	A	N	B	L	A	N	K	E	T	N	T	E
N	S	T	A	Y	M	E	H	W	R	W	F	A	E	B
T	H	R	I	V	O	E	A	P	B	I	F	P	K	X
E	S	W	B	N	E	N	V	I	I	N	H	S	N	D
E	H	A	T	E	C	R	E	S	N	G	O	A	I	S
N	A	I	S	I	L	U	S	T	K	I	T	C	F	T
I	V	S	P	C	N	T	P	K	I	T	S	K	E	R
F	E	T	O	D	I	T	T	Y	B	A	G	T	R	E
E	R	B	O	N	S	C	A	B	B	A	R	D	S	D
F	S	E	N	N	M	G	F	P	R	A	R	E	O	B
C	O	L	C	A	R	T	R	I	D	G	E	B	O	X
T	C	T	P	R	S	T	C	C	D	G	X	X	T	B
M	K	S	H	O	S	H	O	C	A	P	B	O	X	V

EQUIPMENT

WAIST BELT	KNIFE	BAYONET
SEWING	KIT	SPOON
CARTRIDGE BOX	CANTEEN	CAP BOX
TIN CUP	DITTY BAG	KNAPSACK
HAVERSACK	BLANKET	SCABBARD

MATCH THE PEOPLE WITH THE ACTIVITY FOR WHICH THEY ARE FAMOUS

1. John Brown
2. Harriett Tubman
3. Fredrick Douglass
4. David Farragut
5. John Ericcson
6. Clara Barton
7. Louisa May Alcott
8. Emmeline Piggot
9. Julia Ward Howe
10. Loreta Janeta Velazquez

A. Author of Little Women
B. Posed as Southern Lieutenant Harry Buford
C. Abolitionist
D. Union Admiral
E. Ran Underground Railroad
F. Author of "Battle Hymn of the Republic"
G. Inventor/Engineer
H. Organized American Red Cross
I. Author of Uncle's Tom Cabin
J. Famous Confederate Spy

MATCH THE BATTLE WITH THE STATE IN WHICH IT TOOK PLACE

1. Fort Sumter
2. Bull Run
3. Shiloh
4. Antietam
5. Chancellorsville
6. Gettysburg
7. Vicksburg
8. Chickamauga
9. Wilderness
10. Atlanta

A. Maryland
B. Tennessee
C. Tennessee
D. South Carolina
E. Pennsylvania
F. Virginia
G. Mississippi
H. Virginia
I. Georgia
J. Virginia

NORTH OR SOUTH MATCH-UP

Next to each word (or words), fill-in with either an "N" (for North) or an "S" (for South) as it applies.

1. Dixie ___

2. Bonnie Blue Flag ___

3. Blue Uniform ___

4. Rebel Yell ___

5. Billy Yank ___

6. Confederate ___

7. Union ___

8. Federal ___

9. Gray Uniform ___

10. General Grant ___

11. General Lee ___

12. Abe Lincoln ___

13. Jefferson Davis ___

14. Yankee Doodle ___

Puzzles, Games, Codes and More!   - 115 -   **Chapter 11**

T	I	J	H	H	N	E	N	O	U	A	T	N	N	G
I	T	U	O	U	J	N	T	U	A	D	L	R	T	R
M	R	O	Y	J	I	I	R	S	S	R	P	O	R	T
N	G	P	I	Y	T	T	C	T	S	T	O	W	S	G
A	L	S	Y	W	H	T	S	R	O	S	S	T	O	D
H	P	D	E	S	J	J	T	E	U	O	R	N	U	E
C	S	R	T	A	B	I	U	D	O	L	T	N	P	O
A	T	T	T	R	I	B	O	C	U	P	G	L	L	P
L	R	E	R	T	U	U	J	F	N	U	H	C	T	L
O	G	A	M	O	K	E	N	G	Q	I	N	U	Y	S
I	L	B	C	P	E	K	F	H	W	N	M	E	H	A
N	O	N	E	N	R	E	G	O	D	G	G	Y	F	C
O	N	M	U	M	T	R	P	H	R	O	E	D	B	
L	M	X	P	C	G	N	S	R	O	C	D	W	P	H

Find the message hidden above by circling every third letter starting with the upper left-hand letter. You must place the punctuation in the correct place in order to understand the message. Good luck!

_____

_____

_____

_____

ANAGRAMS

An anagram is a word or phrase formed by transposing the letters of another word or phrase. For example, you can make over fifteen different words (three or more letters each) from the word "sport": top, rot, sort, port, tops, rots, spot, stop, pot, pots, sop, sot, strop, post, ports, pro, pros, opt, and opts.

Using the letters in the following words, set the timer for three minutes in order to see how many words (of three or more letters each) that you can make. If a letter is only listed once in the word, then you may only use it once in each new word you form. If a certain letter is used more than once in the word listed, then you may use it as often as it appears.

As a variation to the above rules, play this game with a group. After the time has expired have each player call out the words which they have found. Each player should eliminate any words that are not verifiable from a dictionary, as well as words which other players have duplicated. The object of this game is to be the one with the most original words remaining on your list.

CONFEDERATE   REBELLION

GETTYSBURG   SURRENDER

SOLDIERS   APPOMATTOX

FEDERALS   WASHINGTON

Over 50 words can be made from most of the words listed above, and several can be made into over 100 different words.

WORD JUMBLES

See how quickly you can unscramble the words listed below. If you wish, this can be played in groups as they compete against each other in order to determine which group first unscrambles the words correctly. Remember, the unscrambled words pertain in some way to the Civil War period. (No, the second word is not "shout." Try again.)

TNROH

UHOST

GTFHI

ETLABT

NCLLINO

CDEESE

DCMIHRNO

RNDACIOL

GNSOWHANIT

RALVCYA

GIMNEETR

CMIEAPANNTOI

MDBBARONTEM

GUDNDNURREO

ANSWER TO PUZZLE ON PAGE 101

TOMORROW WE WILL MARCH TO SHILOH.

BE PREPARED AT FIRST LIGHT.

MAKE SURE YOU HAVE YOUR PROVISIONS.

ANSWER TO PUZZLE ON PAGE 102

MOSES IS GOING INTO EGYPT.

THE RAILROAD IS ON ITS WAY.

LISTEN FOR THE SONGS TO LEAD THE WAY.

ANSWER TO PUZZLE ON PAGE 103

HARRIET IS HIDING IN NEW YORK.

SHE IS FREEING THE SLAVES.

THERE IS A HUGE REWARD FOR HER CAPTURE.

Puzzles, Games, Codes and More!

Chapter 11

ANSWER TO PUZZLE ON PAGE 104

U	N	I	O	N	A	D	F	G	E	N	E	R	A	L	X
A	O	T	S	D	V	G	E	D	I	V	I	S	I	O	N
T	R	O	O	F	S	E	D	A	V	I	S	S	Y	I	V
L	T	M	U	R	G	N	E	R	R	C	L	I	T	S	C
P	H	S	N	O	G	R	A	N	T	A	U	R	S	S	I
C	E	C	A	B	I	N	A	I	T	P	V	F	A	U	V
P	W	O	L	E	I	L	L	H	L	E	T	B	U	E	I
G	U	N	I	R	L	L	I	R	U	I	S	A	U	L	L
E	C	F	N	T	S	I	S	O	N	N	I	U	R	S	W
T	S	E	C	E	D	E	T	A	S	C	E	M	T	U	A
R	R	D	R	L	W	T	S	D	C	O	T	T	O	N	R
O	V	E	E	A	A	P	O	L	R	E	N	C	V		
O	L	R	B	E	T	U	B	M	A	N	N	R	N	L	F
P	T	A	T	E	C	B	A	N	D	C	D	T	R	E	R
S	E	T	B	M	L	L	T	Y	V	I	C	T	O	R	Y
L	N	E	P	A	B	E	B	A	T	T	L	E	Y	S	L

ANSWER TO PUZZLE ON PAGE 105

S	H	I	L	O	H	H	I	L	R	G	M	T
N	S	H	A	R	P	S	B	U	R	G	M	O
T	A	V	E	F	T	S	U	M	T	E	R	
A	N	T	I	E	T	A	M	C	K	S	R	X
G	T	Y	S	C	B	R	G	E	L	P	R	M
M	A	N	M	E	K	B	U	L	P	P	I	O
Y	E	G	M	N	I	S	T	R	P	G	M	N
P	G	E	T	T	Y	S	B	U	R	G	A	I
J	U	N	B	U	L	L	R	U	N	O	C	T
M	A	N	A	S	S	A	S	E	R	X	K	O
P	M	N	T	I	R	O	S	J	K	G	P	R
X	B	A	P	P	O	M	A	T	T	O	X	T
M	T	L	O	F	J	U	N	C	T	I	O	N

Puzzles, Games, Codes and More! — 120 — **Chapter 11**

ANSWER TO PUZZLE ON PAGE 106

	D	A	V	I	S		H			S
	P						A			U
H	P						Y			M
O	O			A			F	O	R	T
U	M	O	N	I	T	O	R			E
G	R	A	N	T			O			R
H	T			I			T	R	Y	
	T			E			E			Y
	O			T			B			E
	A	X		A			E			L
	B			M			L			L
L	E	E								

ANSWER TO PUZZLE ON PAGE 107

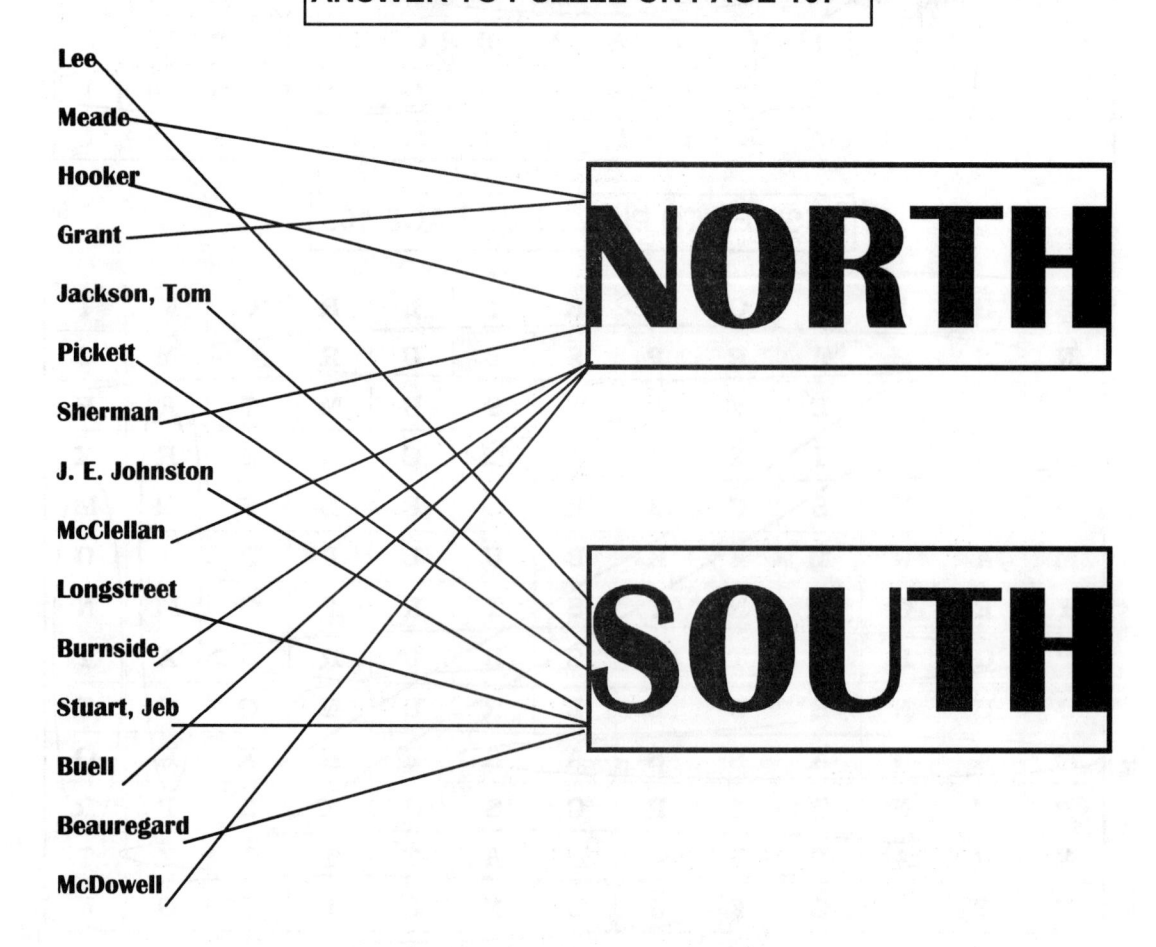

Lee — NORTH/SOUTH
Meade — NORTH
Hooker — NORTH
Grant — NORTH
Jackson, Tom — SOUTH
Pickett — SOUTH
Sherman — NORTH
J. E. Johnston — SOUTH
McClellan — NORTH
Longstreet — SOUTH
Burnside — NORTH
Stuart, Jeb — SOUTH
Buell — NORTH
Beauregard — SOUTH
McDowell — NORTH

Puzzles, Games, Codes and More! — **Chapter 11**

ANSWER TO PUZZLE ON PAGE 108

G	N	T	C	A	N	N	O	N	S
A	M	G	S	Y	N	H	U	R	T
F	O	R	T	P	L	R	T	S	U
M	M	A	S	T	N	O	R	T	H
O	R	N	H	F	G	S	L	H	H
L	E	T	N	U	O	G	L	F	S
A	G	T	S	O	U	T	H	G	A
R	M	Y	E	E	T	G	R	L	Y
M	N	O	U	T	S	F	L	A	G
Y	R	L	E	E	F	G	G	U	T

ANSWER TO PUZZLE ON PAGE 109

1. The third state to secede from the Union. FL<u>O</u>RIDA

2. Billy Yank's nemesis. JOHNNY RE<u>B</u>

3. The noise made famous by the South. <u>R</u>EBEL YELL

4. The second speaker at Gettysburg. L<u>I</u>NCOLN

5. First Northern ironclad. MO<u>N</u>ITOR

6. South's favorite general. L<u>E</u>E

7. Location first firing of war took place. FORT SUMT<u>E</u>R

8. Harriet Tubman's underground. RAI<u>L</u>ROAD

9. Second location of Southern capital. R<u>I</u>CHMOND

War of REBELLION

Puzzles, Games, Codes and More!

- 122 -

Chapter 11

ANSWER TO PUZZLE ON PAGE 109

B	A	Y	O	N	E	T	A	T	C	V	F	R	L
O	W	A	R	N	E	Y	P	I	A	T	S	L	R
W	S	R	A	M	M	E	R	W	R	I	F	L	E
I	H	R	A	M	R	E	V	P	B	S	F	T	V
E	S	H	F	U	M	R	S	I	I	H	F	H	O
K	L	O	A	T	U	V	T	S	N	L	O	E	L
N	M	W	M	U	S	K	E	T	E	S	L	R	V
I	R	I	I	C	K	T	L	O	I	T	S	S	E
F	A	T	N	A	R	C	U	L	B	E	T	T	R
E	M	Z	I	N	A	A	A	W	A	B	E	L	S
F	R	E	E	N	M	G	F	N	R	A	R	E	O
E	O	R	U	H	S	U	H	W	N	R	S	U	U
T	D	K	S	T	T	N	T	A	C	O	T	O	T
M	D	S	H	O	S	H	O	T	G	U	N	N	H

ANSWER TO PUZZLE ON PAGE 111

C	A	B	O	N	E	T	A	T	C	S	F	K	L	A
A	W	H	A	N	B	L	A	N	K	E	T	N	T	E
N	S	T	A	Y	M	E	H	W	R	W	F	A	E	B
T	H	R	I	V	O	E	A	P	B	I	F	P	K	X
E	S	W	B	N	E	N	V	I	I	N	H	S	N	D
E	H	A	T	E	C	R	E	S	N	G	O	A	I	S
N	A	I	S	I	L	U	S	T	K	I	T	C	F	T
I	V	S	P	C	N	T	P	K	I	T	S	K	E	R
F	E	T	O	D	I	T	T	Y	B	A	G	T	R	E
E	R	B	O	N	S	C	A	B	B	A	R	D	S	D
F	S	E	N	M	G	F	P	R	A	R	E	O	B
O	A	L	C	A	R	T	R	I	D	G	E	B	O	X
T	C	T	S	T	T	N	T	A	C	O	T	O	T	B
M	K	S	H	O	S	H	O	C	A	P	B	O	X	V

Puzzles, Games, Codes and More! — Chapter 11

ANSWER TO PUZZLE ON PAGE 112

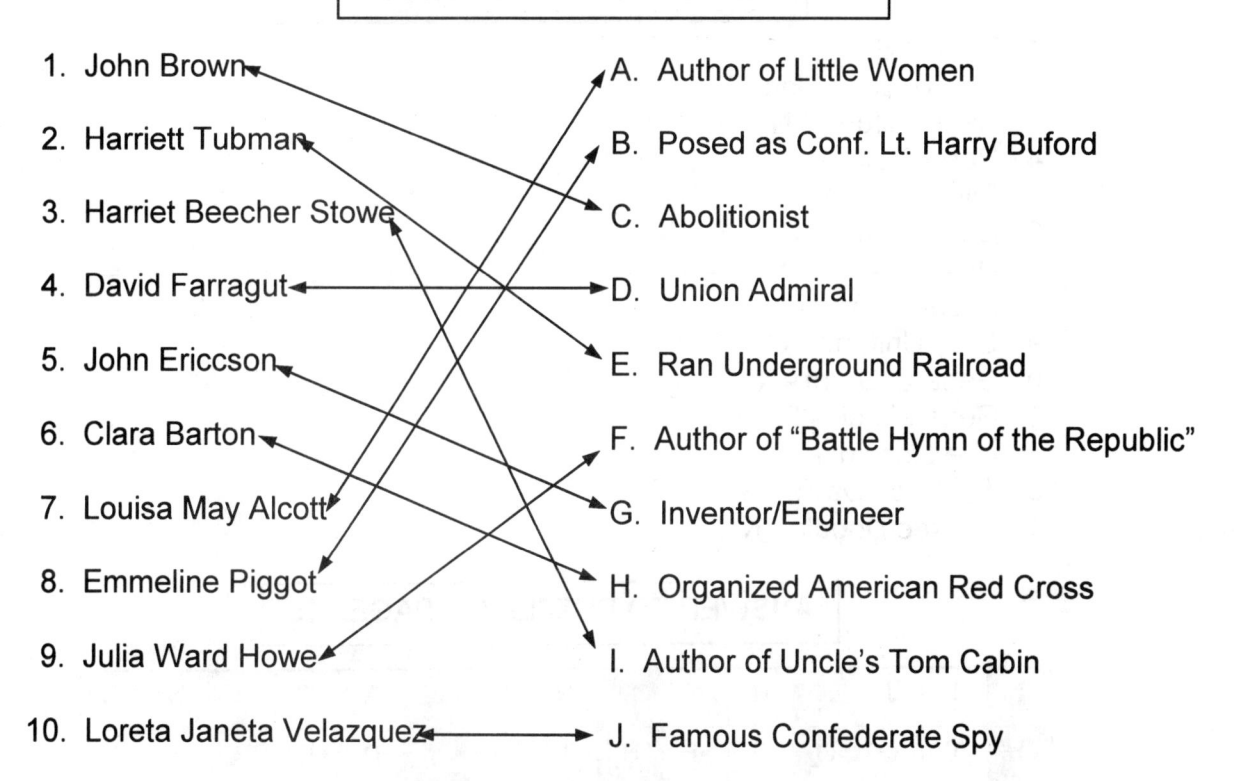

1. John Brown — C. Abolitionist
2. Harriett Tubman — E. Ran Underground Railroad
3. Harriet Beecher Stowe — I. Author of Uncle's Tom Cabin
4. David Farragut — D. Union Admiral
5. John Ericcson — G. Inventor/Engineer
6. Clara Barton — H. Organized American Red Cross
7. Louisa May Alcott — A. Author of Little Women
8. Emmeline Piggot — J. Famous Confederate Spy
9. Julia Ward Howe — F. Author of "Battle Hymn of the Republic"
10. Loreta Janeta Velazquez — B. Posed as Conf. Lt. Harry Buford

ANSWER TO PUZZLE ON PAGE 113

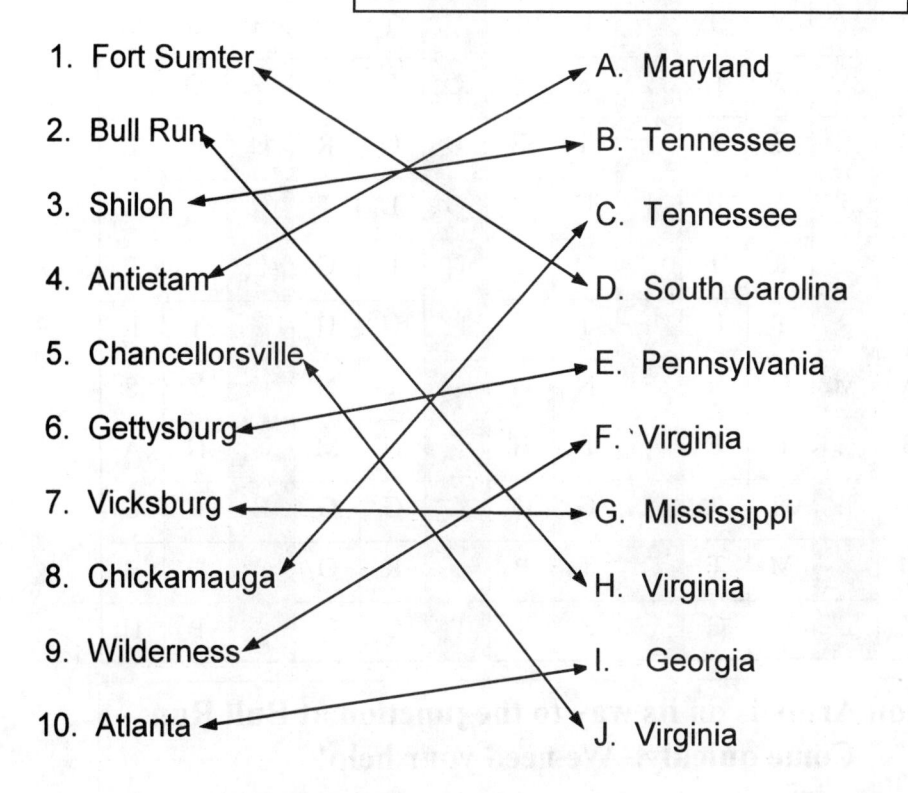

1. Fort Sumter — D. South Carolina
2. Bull Run — F. Virginia
3. Shiloh — C. Tennessee
4. Antietam — A. Maryland
5. Chancellorsville — H. Virginia
6. Gettysburg — E. Pennsylvania
7. Vicksburg — G. Mississippi
8. Chickamauga — B. Tennessee
9. Wilderness — J. Virginia
10. Atlanta — I. Georgia

Puzzles, Games, Codes and More!

Chapter 11

ANSWER TO PUZZLE ON PAGE 114

1. Dixie - S
2. Bonnie Blue Flag - S
3. Blue Uniform - N
4. Rebel Yell - S
5. Billy Yank - N
6. Confederate - S
7. Union - N
8. Federal - N
9. Gray Uniform - S
10. General Grant - N
11. General Lee - S
12. Abe Lincoln - N
13. Jefferson Davis - S
14. Yankee Doodle - N

ANSWER TO PUZZLE ON PAGE 115

T	I	J	H	H	N	E	N	O	U	A	T	N	N	G
I	T	U	O	U	J	N	T	U	A	D	L	R	T	R
M	R	O	Y	J	I	I	R	S	S	R	P	O	R	T
N	G	P	I	Y	T	T	C	T	S	T	O	W	S	G
A	L	S	Y	W	H	T	S	R	O	S	S	T	O	D
H	P	D	E	S	J	J	T	E	U	O	R	N	U	E
C	S	R	T	A	B	I	U	D	O	L	T	N	P	O
A	T	T	T	R	I	B	O	C	U	P	G	L	L	P
L	R	E	R	T	U	U	J	F	N	U	H	C	T	L
O	G	A	M	O	K	E	N	G	Q	I	N	U	Y	S
I	L	B	C	P	E	K	F	H	L	N	M	Y	H	A
W	O	N	E	N	R	G	O	E	G	G	E	F	C	
D	N	M	Y	M	T	O	T	P	U	R	O	R	D	B
H	M	X	E	C	G	L	S	R	P	C	D	!	P	H

The Union Army is on its way to the junction at Bull Run. Come quickly. We need your help!

| Puzzles, Games, Codes and More! | - 125 - | Chapter 11 |

ANSWER TO PUZZLE ON PAGE 116

Since there are over 1,000 possible words to be made from the list of words on page 95, I am not going to include the answer to the anagrams. If you have access to a an electronic wordmaster (such as made by Franklin®), enter a word under "Word Builder" and the wordmaster will then provide you with a list of all the words that can be made from the word you entered.

ANSWER TO PUZZLE ON PAGE 117

1. North
2. South
3. Fight
4. Battle
5. Lincoln
6. Secede
7. Richmond
8. Ironclad
9. Washington
10. Calvary
11. Regiment
12. Emancipation
13. Bombardment
14. Underground

FIELDTRIPS AND ACTIVITIES
Chapter 12

The fieldtrips and activities portion of this unit study is the part which children will find most enjoyable. Depending on where you live in the United States, fieldtrips can range from being relatively easy to nearly impossible. If fieldtrips are not feasible for you, there are plenty of other ativities you can create for your students that will help them achieve a feel for what life during the Civil War was like.

Your first assignment is to research the part that your state (or any state located near your state) played in the Civil War. We live in Florida, and although there were no major battles which took place here, there were a few noteworthy skirmishes. There are also several museums, forts, and prisons to visit, all within a 150 mile radius of our home. There are at least five reenactments planned each year in Florida. *The Camp Chase Gazette* (listed in the bibliography) is an excellent source for learning the date and location of scheduled Civil War reenactments. Also, listed in the bibliography is an wonderful book entitled *Civil War Parks — The story behind the Scenery* (William C. "Jack" Davis, KC Publications, Inc., 1992). The full color photography in this books will make you want to visit every site listed.

We attended a reenactment during our study of the Civil War, and the children are still talking about everything that they saw and heard. Through a series of unrelated events, we met a park ranger living in our town who was a reenactor and is a descendant of a soldier who participated in a local battle. We arranged for him to come in costume to the location of the battle and share with the children information concerning this battle. Additionally, a friend of this park ranger, also a reenactor and a photographer, joined us there. He helped a homeschool student take black and white pictures (in order to look authentic to the period) of the children dressed in costume. We thoroughly enjoyed ourselves and learned a great deal. Incidentally, those photographs are the ones displayed on the cover and throughout this volume.

The Museum of Florida History also has a display of Civil War memorabilia. Our state library has newspapers on micro-fiche that date back to the Civil War period, and the older children were able to view

Fieldtrips and Activities   - 128 -   **Chapter 12**

these documents.

Dressing the children in costume, as mentioned above, was one of the highlights of the study. Knowing that the pictures were going to be taken with black and white film, we didn't worry about the color of the costumes. Basically, we "threw together" coats, sashes, hats, boots, etc., from our closets, or found them quite inexpensively at garage sales and thrift stores. To put insignias, rank, and stripes on the pants, shirts and jackets, we simply used thin masking tape. No sewing was required, and this too was very inexpensive.

One of the parents in our study group has a friend who owns an authentic sword and some other equipment used in the Civil War. She was able to borrow these to share with the children. By word of mouth you should be able to track down many interesting items to share with your class as well. Contact your local Chamber of Commerce and your State Department of Tourism for information pertaining to your area. If you aren't able to subscribe to the *Camp Chase Gazette*, maybe you can order a recent issue for the information on reenactments. Bob Farewell of Lifetime Books and Gifts puts on an excellent workshop entitled "The Second Day of Gettysburg." If he is going to be in your area, talk him into giving this presentation for your group.

The following pages list tourist information on each state, provided by *Facts Plus* (page 102), written by Susan C. Anthony. Subsequent to the tourist information, a few ideas and activities are suggested for your group to pursue.

Megan Purvis

Fieldtrips and Activities — Chapter 12

Alabama	1-800-ALABAMA (out-of-state callers only)
Alaska	1-907-465-2010
Arizona	1-602-542-8687
Arkansas	1-800-NATURAL
California	1-800-862-2543
Colorado	1-800-433-2656
Connecticut	1-800-CT BOUND
Delaware	1-800-441-8846
District of Columbia	1-202-789-7000
Florida	1-904-487-1462
Georgia	1-800-VISIT GA
Hawaii	1-808-586-2550
Idaho	1-800-635-7820
Illinois	1-800-223-0121
Indiana	1-800-289-6646
Iowa	1-800-345-IOWA
Kansas	1-800-2KANSAS
Kentucky	1-800-225-TRIP
Louisiana	1-800-33-GUMBO
Maine	1-800-533-9595 (out-of-state callers only)
Maryland	1-800-543-1036
Massachusetts	1-800-624-MASS
Michigan	1-800--543-2937
Minnesota	1-800-328-1461
Mississippi	1-800-647-2290 (out-of-state callers only)
Missouri	1-800-877-1234
Montana	1-800-541-1447
Nebraska	1-800-228-4307 (out-of-state callers only)
Nevada	1-800-638-2328
New Hampshire	1-603-271-2666
New Jersey	1-800-JERSEY-7
New Mexico	1-800-545-2040
New York	1-800-CALLNYS
North Carolina	1-800-VISITING
North Dakota	1-800-437-2077
Ohio	1-800-BUCKEYE
Oklahoma	1-800-652-6552
Oregon	1-800-547-7842 (out-of-state callers only)
Pennsylvania	1-800-VISITPA
Rhode Island	1-800-556-2484
South Carolina	1-803-734-0135
South Dakota	1-800-843-1930 (out-of-state callers only)

Fieldtrips and Activities - 130 - **Chapter 12**

Tennessee	1-615-741-1904
Texas	1-512-462-9191
Utah	1-801-538-1030
Vermont	1-802-828-3236
Virginia	1-800-VISITVA
Washington	1-800-544-1800
West Virginia	1-800-CALLWVA
Wisconsin	1-800-372-2737
Wyoming	1-800-CALLWYO

Stacey Wesolowski

Scout, Search and Find

One of the things which amazed me in the study of the Civil War was the huge number of miles these armies covered, many times not even traveling on roads. Although hundreds and hundreds of miles were covered, these armies found each other! Part of this was due to the scouts, spies and cavalry, but there were many times where one army was at a huge disadvantage not knowing the location of the enemy. This game will help your students get a feel for how frustrating this must have been.

Your mission: Find the enemy before they find you!

Divide your group into two teams. If you aren't conducting this unit study with a group, then recruit enough friends to play so you can form two teams. One team will wear gray arm bands (representing the South) and the other team will wear blue arm bands (representing the North).

Go to a safe, wooded area and designate a spot out of the woods as the "fort." Give one team a ten-minute head start, instructing them to stay together (at least in pairs) but hide as well as they can. After ten minutes, blow a whistle as an announcement that the other team will begin searching for the hidden team. The object of the game is for a majority of the hidden team to get back to the fort before being sighted by the other team. When the team that is searching sees any member of the hidden team <u>before</u> they get to the fort, then they are allowed to "capture" that member. If a majority of the hidden team gets to the fort before being sighted, then they are the victors.

As a variation, and if everyone is agreement, each side can pick one "scout" who can remain uncaptured as they spy on the movements of the other army. Also, instead of capturing by sight, each team could wear strips of material from their waistband that the enemy has to secure in order to capture that soldier.

Play several rounds, taking turns between the team that hides and the team that searches. Keep score and see if the outcome of your "war" is different from the Civil War!

Let's Go on a Scavenger Hunt!

This activity can either be done at a library (preferably during morning hours when it isn't too busy) or at any other location where a selection of reference books are available. Divide your students into two teams and have them pick a regiment (from a list that you have already prepared) which actually participated in the Civil War. Hand out identical sheets requesting the information listed below, and see which team can "hunt and find" the desired facts first.

1. In how many total battles did this regiment participate?
2. What were the largest battles in which they fought?
3. Who were the leaders in charge of this regiment?
4. How many of the battles in which they fought did they win?
5. What was the total number of men involved in this regiment?
6. How many soldiers from this regiment were wounded or killed in battle?
7. Plot the geographic course of the regiment's participation in the war.
8. Who are the most well-known men involved with this regiment?

Richard & Jeffrey Barnard

Millie Barnard

Fieldtrips and Activities **Chapter 12**

While You're at the Library . . .

First check with your local library, then state and/or university libraries until you find one that has newspapers on micro-fiche that date as far back as the 1860's. Check also with your local newspaper to find out if they have access to papers that were published during the Civil War. Once you locate a place which has the newspapers on file, find out their policy on using and making copies of the material you need. Our state library does have newspapers which date back this far, and they allowed us to use their micro-fiche viewers and make copies at no charge.

Once you find a location for the papers, if it is within travelling distance, then plan a field trip! It would be advantageous to teach your students how to use a micro-fiche viewer before your trip, but this isn't necessary as most will learn quite readily after watching someone else operate the machine a few times.

If you are allowed to make copies, get a wide variety of entries, such as obituaries, want ads, recipes, classified ads, editorials, and cartoons. Also have your students take note of the names and the prices of the newspapers published during the Civil War period.

Jonathan Wesolowski

CIVIL WAR QUESTIONS
Chapter 13

Although I am not a big fan of the "chew-up-and-spit-out" technique as a means for learning and retaining information, having your students participate in a "Quiz Bowl" is a great way for them to find out how much they have learned and retained. Most children enjoy competition and as a finale to your unit study, a quiz bowl is a lot of fun. Divide the students into groups. How many groups you have will depend on the number of children participating. Another option is to divide boys against girls or students against parent/teachers. If you have access to equipment that will allow the children to "buzz in" (like on Jeopardy), it makes the competition even more fun. The questions below are provided for your convenience. It may be preferable for you to create your own questions, knowing better the material your students have covered. An answer key to the following questions is included for your benefit as well.

1. Who was the President immediately preceding President Lincoln?
2. Who became President when President Lincoln was shot and killed?
3. Who was the President of the South?
4. In what city was the Southern capital first located?
5. Who killed Abraham Lincoln?
6. Who killed John Wilkes Booth?
7. What was the occupation of John Wilkes Booth?
8. Where was the Southern capital moved?
9. Who was the most famous of the Southern generals?
10. After the Civil War, which Northern general was first elected President?
11. At what fort was the first shot of the Civil War fired?
12. What month and year did the firing on Fort Sumter first take place?
13. Who was killed when the Southerners took over Fort Sumter?
14. How was Daniel Hough killed at Ft. Sumter?

Quiz Bowl Questions — Chapter 13

15. Where did the first major battle of the Civil War take place?

16. Who was the Northern general at Manassas?

17. What were the names of the first two ironclads that battled?

18. In what state did the battle of Shiloh take place?

19. Which Southern general was killed at the battle of Shiloh?

20. Who were the Northern generals involved at Shiloh?

21. What is the name of the orders which were lost by one of Lee's generals prior to the Battle of Antietam?

22. What Northern general was in charge at the Battle of Antietam?

23. In what state did the Battle of Antietam take place?

24. What Northern general was famous for burning Atlanta?

25. Who shot Stonewall Jackson?

26. What is the name of a famous Southern prison in Georgia which housed thousands of Northern prisoners?

27. What is the name of the book Victor Hugo wrote and published in 1862?

28. What woman is famous for her part in the Underground Railroad?

29. Who wrote *Uncle Tom's Cabin*?

30. What color did the Northern troops commonly wear?

31. What color did the Southern troops commonly wear?

32. When was the Emancipation Proclamation to take effect?

33. What speech is President Lincoln famous?

34. How does the Gettysburg Address begin?

35. Which battle was the turning point of the war, giving the North a distinct advantage when the South lost hope of Europe helping them?

36. Which battle was responsible for changing the nature of naval battle?

37. In what state did the Battle of Gettysburg take place?

38. In what state did the Battle of Manassas/Bull Run take place?

39. In what state is Wilson's Creek?

40. What is the official name given to the Civil War?

41. What do most Southerners prefer the Civil War be called?

42. John Rowlands, the deserter both to the South and then to the North is more famous for these words, "Dr. Livingstone, I presume?" What is his better known alias (or other name)?

43. What was wrapped around three cigars and found by two Federal soldiers, which cost Lee the Battle of Antietam?

44. Which battle suffered the most casualties?

45. Who was Daniel Tarbox?

46. Who was Wade Hampton?

47. For what is Matthew Brady famous?

48. Where is Ft. Pulaski located?

49. What famous organization was formed with the help of Clara Barton, a nurse during the Civil War?

50. How did the Civil War officially end?

51. Where did the surrender take place?

52. What fort is located near Pensacola, Florida?

53. Where was the Rebel Yell first heard?

54. If you were too young to fight but wanted to join the army, how could you serve?

55. Who do many think could have won the Battle of Gettysburg for the South had he still been alive?

56. Where did Stonewall Jackson get his nickname?

57. Which battle is Jackson credited for his greatest victory?

58. How did Jackson die?

59. What is an ironclad?

60. What do the surveillance balloon and submarine have in common?

61. What is a "sutler"?

62. About how many words are in the Gettysburg Address?

63. Who gave the Gettysburg Address?

64. What was the general opinion of the Gettysburg Address immediately after the ceremony?

65. At whose house did the surrender in Appomatox take place?

66. What is a "run," as in "Bull Run"?

67. What is the cavalry?

68. Who was the famous cavalry leader for the South?

69. When did Lee become infuriated because of Stuart's inability to return and report on movements of Northern troops in time to help?

70. What was responsible for the largest percentage of deaths during the war?

71. What is Andersonville?

72. To which location did many of the slaves escape?

73. Which state did the North propose be cut in half so the blacks could populate the lower half?

74. Why did some Northerners think the blacks couldn't survive up north?

75. Which two sisters from a prominent South Carolina family fought for the rights of women and the abolition of slavery?

76. What happened to the 53 slaves who seized the Spanish ship, *Amistad*, and sailed to New York State in 1839?

77. Who was the editor of the *Liberator*, an abolitionist newspaper published from 1831 to 1865?

78. Who was the editor of the *North Star* who escaped from slavery in 1838 and earned distinction as an orator, abolitionist, and advocate of women's suffrage?

79. Who was the preacher who instigated a slave uprising in 1831 in Virginia which led to the deaths of fifty-seven whites?

80. Who published the pamphlet in 1829 entitled *Appeal . . . to the Colored People of the World,* which called for worldwide black revolt against white tyranny?

81. Who was the New York news editor who argued that every man had the right to own land and advised his readers to "Go West, young man, go west?"

82. Which proposal appeased opposing factions by admitting California to the Union as a free state, abolished the slave trade in the District of Columbia and established a strong fugitive slave law?

83. Which proposal declared that Cuba should be acquired from Spain, by force if necessary, because the dissolution of slavery in Cuba would

threaten the institution of slavery in the United States?

84. Which proposal intended that all territory gained from Mexico be a place for white settlers to live "without the disgrace which association with Negro slavery brings on white labor"?

85. Which proposal repealed the Missouri Compromise and applied the theory of popular sovereignty to the slavery issue, arguing that the inhabitants of each state should decide whether slavery would be legal in their state?

86. Why was Kansas called "Bleeding Kansas" during the late 1850's?

87. In which 1857 case did the Supreme Court make the following two rulings: (1) freed blacks were not citizens; and (2) the Missouri Compromise was unconstitutional?

88. What state was formed in 1861 by dissidents who refused to secede from the United States?

89. What were the four border states that retained economic and ideological ties to both sides during the Civil War and sent men to fight in both armies?

90. What Northern military strategy contributed to the change in the value of Southern exports after the war began?

91. What two factors contributed to the South's inability to repair damaged locomotives and railroad tracks?

92. What three major ways did the Congress use to raise money for the war effort?

93. How did the Conscription Act of 1863 allow for wealthy people to

escape the draft?

94. What is a "carpetbagger"?

95. What is a "copperhead"?

96. What is a "scalawag"?

97. What is a "sharecropper"?

98. What three actions were the Southern states required to take in order to be readmitted to the Union according to the Reconstruction Act of 1867?

99. Who became the first Black member of Congress in 1870?

100. How did radical republicans in Congress react when President Andrew Johnson tried to block harsh reconstruction legislation?

Allen Gerrell, CSA Reenactor

ANSWER KEY

1. Buchanan
2. Andrew Johnson
3. Jefferson Davis
4. Montgomery, Alabama
5. John Wilkes Booth
6. He was shot and killed on April 26 in a Virginia tobacco barn when soldiers and detectives surrounded and set fire to it.
7. Actor
8. Richmond, Virginia
9. Robert E. Lee
10. Grant
11. Fort Sumter
12. April, 1861
13. Daniel Hough
14. Accidently killed during 100-gun salute at surrender of Fort Sumter
15. Bull Run or Manassas
16. McDowell
17. *Monitor* & *Virginia* (*Merrimac*)
18. Tennessee
19. Johnston
20. Grant, Wallace, Sherman and Buell
21. Special Orders 191
22. General McClellan
23. Maryland
24. Sherman
25. Another Southern soldier
26. Andersonville
27. *Les Miserables*
28. Harriet Tubman
29. Harriet Beecher Stowe
30. Blue
31. Gray
32. January 1863

33. The Gettysburg Address
34. "Four score and seven years ago our fathers . . . ."
35. Antietam
36. The *Monitor* and the *Merrimac*
37. Pennsylvania
38. Virginia
39. Missouri
40. The War of Rebellion
41. The War Between The States
42. Henry M. Stanley
43. Orders 191 (plans of the Southern Army)
44. Gettysburg (51,000)
45. An 18-year-old Northern solder who died at the Battle of Antietam
46. A wealthy S. Carolinian who financed his own troops, "Wade's Legion".
47. His Civil War photographs
48. East coast of Georgia
49. The Red Cross
50. Lee surrendered to Grant first at Appomattox, then other armies followed suit
51. Appomattox
52. Fort Pickens
53. At the 1st Battle of Bull Run
54. Join the band
55. Stonewall Jackson
56. At the Battle of Bull Run
57. Chancellorsville
58. Accidentally shot by his own troops, then developed pneumonia
59. A ship clad with iron plates, railroad ties, etc.
60. Both first used during the Civil War
61. A person following troops to sell food, drink and supplies
62. Approximately 270
63. President Lincoln
64. That it was a failure and would not be remembered by many
65. Major McLean
66. A creek

67. Troops on horses
68. J.E.B. Stuart
69. At the Battle of Gettysburg
70. Disease
71. A major Southern prison located in Georgia
72. Canada
73. Texas
74. Because of the cold weather
75. Angelina and Sarah Grimke
76. Defense attorney John Quincy Adams convinced the Supreme Court to allow them to return to Africa
77. William Lloyd Garrison
78. Frederick Douglass
79. Nat Turner
80. David Walker
81. Horace Greeley
82. Compromise of 1850
83. Ostend Manifesto (1854)
84. Wilmot Proviso (1846-47)
85. Kansas-Nebraska Act (1854)
86. Series of violent confrontations between pro-slavery and anti-slavery settlers
87. The Dred Scott v. Sandford case
88. West Virginia
89. Delaware, Kentucky, Maryland and Missouri
90. The North blockaded Southern ports
91. The South lacked iron and did not have enough factories to produce machinery and supplies vital to the wartime effort.
92. Created a centralized banking system, issued paper money (greenbacks) that was not backed by gold or silver, and levied the first national income tax
93. Men could avoid serving by hiring substitutes to fight in their place or by paying $300 to the government.
94. Northerners who swarmed to the South after the war strictly for financial gain; they apparently were called this because they packed their belongings in the then-popular luggage called "carpetbags"

Quiz Bowl Questions — 145 — Chapter 13

95. Northerners who opposed the war and wanted a peaceful solution — some favored letting the South secede from the North

96. Southern politicians who, after the war, worked with carpetbaggers to gain political power and profit.

97. Poor farmers who tilled land owned by others in exchange for a portion of the product grown

98. To adopt a state constitution that disqualified former Southern officials from holding office; to grant suffrage to black citizens; and to ratify the Fourteenth Amendment

99. Hiram R. Revels

100. They impeached Johnson and tried to remove him from office.

Tony Wesolowski

David Wesolowski

BIBLIOGRAPHY

The books listed in this chapter are recommended for further reading, or can be used by your students when decorating their folders. You may be able to find some of these at your public library. Most of these books can be purchased from the vendors listed below. If the books are not coded with a vendor name, then author and publisher information is provided. Send your catalog requests to:

D. P. & K. Productions (coded as **DP&K**)
2201 High Road
Tallahassee, Florida 32303
(904) 385-1958

A Garden Patch (coded as **GP**)
2353 Woodbend Circle
New Port Richey, FL 34655
(813) 372-7419

Lifetime Books and Gifts (coded as **LBG**)
3900 Chalet Suzanne Dr.
Lake Wales, Florida
1-800-377-0390

R.O.C.K. Solid (coded as **RS**)
3039 Burkit Lane
Jacksonville, FL 32226
1-800-705-3452 or 904-751-3569

* The books noted with an asterisk have been referred to within this study.

Periodicals:

Camp Chase Gazette *
P. O. Box 7078
Marieta, OH 45750
(Bi-monthly magazine; $24/year)

The Civil War News *
Rt. 1 Box 36
Tunbridge, VT 05077
1 (802) 889-3500
(Monthly newsletter; $27/year)

Civil War Times Illustrated *
P. O. Box 1863
Mount Morris, IL 61054-9947
(Bi-monthly magazine; $19.95/year)

Books:

A Defense of Virginia (LBG)
Abe Lincoln - Coloring Book (LBG)
Abe Lincoln - Childhood of a Famous American (LBG)
Abe Lincoln - Sower Series (LBG)
Across five Aprils (LBG)America: First 350 years (LBG)
American Family Civil War Paper Dolls (LBG)
Among the Camps (LBG)
Before Freedom (LBG)
Behind Rebel Lines (LBG)
Black Slodiers of the Civil War - Coloring Book (DP&K)
Christ in the Camp (LBG)
Civil War Encyclopedia *Revised Edition* (Mark Boatner; Random House)*
Civil War Heroes (DP&K, RS)*
Civil War Heroines (DP&K, RS)*

Bibliography — Chapter 14

Civil War Parks - The Story Behind the Scenery (RS)*
Civil War — Strange & Fascinating Facts (Burke Davis; Random House)*
"Co. Aytch" (LBG)*
Coloring Book of the Civil War (DP&K)*
Coming of the Glory (LBG)*
Confederate Manhood - cassette (LBG)
Confederate Trilogy - Live of R. E. Lee,
    Stonewall Jackson and Jeb Stuart (LBG)
Cut and Assemble Southern Plantation (LBG)
Diary of a Southern Refugee (LBG)
Facts the Historians Leave Out (DP&K, LBG)*
Facts Plus (DP&K, LBG)*
Flags of the Civil War — Coloring Book (DP&K)*
From Antietam to Gettysburg (coloring book) (LBG)
Garden Patch of Reproducibles (DP&K, GP, LBG, RS)*
Gettysburg (LBG)
Hard Marching Every Day (LBG)
History of U.S. (boxed set) (LBG)
If You Lived During the Civil War (LBG)
Illustrated Confederate Reader (LBG)*
Iron Scouts of the Confederacy (LBG)
Jackson and Lee - Legends in Gray (LBG)
Killer Angels (LBG) [book on which movie "Gettysburg" was based]
Lee's Last Campaign (LBG)
Lessons from History - 1800's (LBG)
Lost Cause (LBG)
Meet Abraham Lincoln (LBG)
My Folks Don't Want me to Talk About Slavery (LBG)
Nattie's Trip South (LBG)
Ordinary Americans (LBG)
Perilous Road (LBG)
Pink and Say (Patricia Polacco; Scholastic, 1994) *
Rebel (LBG)
Red Badge of Courage & Other Stories (LBG)
Rifles for Watie (LBG)
Robert E. Lee - Young Confederate (LBG)

Bibliography - 150 - **Chapter 14**

Robert E. Lee - Sower Series (LBG)
Shades of Grey (LBG)
Silk Flags and Cold Steel (LBG)
South Was Right (LBG)
Southern By the Grace of God (LBG)
Stonewall Jackson - Sower Series (LBG)
Story of the Civil War Coloring Book (DP&K, & LBG) *
Timetables of History (DP&K, LBG, RS) *
Two Little Confederates (LBG)
Unconditional Surrender: U.S. Grant (LBG)
War For What? (LBG)

Kelley Wesolowski